MW00779071

"SONRISE"

"FATHER AND MOTHER I LOVE YOU"

A STORY

BY

S. TERRY LEWIS

It is with great pleasure that I dedicate this book to Carmen Smith, Senior Vice President at Disney, who not only suggested that I write this story as a screenplay but provided me with materials to get started. Carmen is one of my wife, Barbara's, closest and dearest friends.

■■

I first want to recognize Amanda Barnes, Writing Assistant. After a couple of major disappointments and some confusion early on, the project, which consisted of converting a screenplay to book format and then to Audible, was about to be canceled, but Amanda convinced me to give her a chance with the project.

Amanda is a Blessing with a winning personality, excellent writing skills, and vision. Working with her was as much of a pleasure as seeing my words come to life in the characters of this story.
I look forward to working with her again in the near future.

Rap segment:
'Do for yours'
by Sli.

Table of Contents

Chapter 1 - The phenomenon

A panel of representatives from five New York schools, one from each borough, is seated at a large polished mahogany table with high-backed chairs, sipping coffee and making small talk. There is Ms. Andrews, an attractive blonde woman about thirty who has been teaching seventh-grade Mathematics for a year now. In the same room, there is Mrs. Brooks, who is thirty-eight years old, but her choice of eyeglasses makes her look much older. With the look of a secretary, Mrs. Brooks teaches Social Studies. Then there is Mr. Edwards wearing a shirt with sleeves rolled once, slightly bald, and a pencil behind his ear. He is forty years old and an Art teacher. On the other side of the table is Ms. Clark, a middle-aged, stout black woman with a baby face who teaches Language Arts. Next to her sits Ms. Daniels, a thirty-five-year-old, brunette Computer Science teacher by profession, smartly dressed in a very business look. At the opposite end of the table sits Mr. Fisher, a family advocate by profession. The seat at the head of the table is empty. A cluster of glasses, some napkins, and a pitcher of water are placed in the center of the table. Manila folders have been placed on the table in front of each chair. A computer and a telephone sit on a desk in one corner.

The room is large, with a dark gray carpet and white walls embellished with a picture of the mayor on one wall and a large picture of the World Trade Towers emblazoned with the American Flag on the opposite wall. Several plaques and citations give the room an official look. Cranberry drapes frame a large picture window, providing plenty of sunlight and a great view of part of the uptown skyline and part of the East River. As ferries and tugboats make their way slowly up and down the river, you can see the borough of Queens on the other side.

The conference room door is open, people are seen passing, and the sounds of the elevator chimes, and people laughing, talking, and greeting each other can be heard. Education and a distinguished-looking gentleman of about fifty with gray around the temples and a loud, booming voice, appears at the door. Dressed in a gray suit, he stops and turns to his left when he hears someone call him.

He sees Lina Matalwis, his secretary, a beautiful Latino woman of about twenty, carrying a clipboard and walking towards him.

"Would you sign these, please, Mr. Dawson?" Lina asks him, handing him the clipboard.

He takes the clipboard, signs the top page, folds it back, signs a second document, folds two more pages back, and signs a third.

In a soft voice, unusual for him, he tells her, "Make sure that these go out right away, Lina, and hurry back."

Taking the clipboard, she replies, "Yes, sir, I will," and walks away hurriedly as Dawson watches her.

With that task done, he enters the room and, in his usual booming voice, greets, "Good morning!" to everyone seated.

As the panel returns his greeting, he takes his seat at the head of the table and looks at the panel seated at his left and right.

"Shall we get started?" he asks everyone as Lina returns. The panel responds with a "Yes, sir," and they open their folders.

"What you have in front of you, sir, are the reading scores of 94 students as of the close of school in June and the scores from the battery of tests given two weeks ago," says Miss. Andrews. "As you can see, sir, the scores have changed dramatically."

Dawson, holding one page in each hand while looking back and forth, replies, "Umm...hmm...interesting...very interesting. Could these scores be the result of test grading errors?"

"No, sir. The tests were graded under standard conditions by a team of graders," replies Miss. Andrews. Some students were even tested twice. Twelve children at my school, IS61 in Queens, have increased their reading scores in the past seven months. Seven of these children had increases of two grade levels, and five had increases of three grade levels."

"There were eight cases reported at my school, sir, with increases of three grade levels," adds Miss. Brooks.

"Which school do you represent, Miss. Brooks? Dawson asks her.

"Sorry, sir, PS118 in the Bronx," she replies.

"We have ten cases at PS209 in Staten Island. Six with increases of two grade levels and four with increases of three grade levels," adds Ms. Clark.

Miss. Daniels, too, speaks up, stating, "My school, PS74 in Bed Stuy., Brooklyn, reports nine cases with increases of two grade levels."

"It's happening all over the city, sir," Mr. Edwards concludes. "There have been 94 cases of academic acceleration reported from seventeen schools in the five boroughs. My school, IS10, in Manhattan, reports five cases. One child had an increase of one grade level, and the other four children had increases of three grade levels."

Scratching his head in thought, Dawson asks, "And all of these children's reading levels increased so drastically within a period of only seven months?"

"All within the past seven months, yes, sir," confirms Mr. Edwards.

"In all my thirty-two years as an educator, I have never heard of anything like this happening," Dawson states.

"With all due respect, sir, that's not quite true," Mr. Fisher speaks up. "Remember when the law was passed to take prayer out of the schools and to delete the word "God" from the pledge of allegiance? After that, a significant percentage of student behavior, attention span, and grades took a turn for the worse. This is like the same thing in reverse."

"He's right," Miss. Andrews seconds him. "Before that was done, we never had teachers being assaulted or students bringing guns to school and killing teachers and other students. When prayer was taken out of the schools, things really did take a turn for the worse."

"You're right. Now that I think about it, you're right," agrees Dawson.

"Be that as it may, prayer is still not allowed, but these students' reading scores are up, and their attendance and behavior have improved also," adds Miss. Brooks. "That's not all; there has been an increase in the number of black parents in attendance at PTA meetings as well."

"Are these all black children?" Dawson asks.

"Yes, sir," replies Ms. Clark.

"Have any of the parents of these children been questioned?" Dawson asks. "No doubt they have some answers."

At that statement, the teachers look at each other as if they are hiding something.

Hesitantly, Miss. Andrews speaks up, "As a matter of fact, sir, uh—"

Anxious, Dawson interrupts sarcastically, "Well, what is it? What is it?"

"We've talked to just about all of the parents, and we've found that they have something very strange in common," informs Miss. Brooks.

"Well, are you going to tell me what it is, or do I have to choke it out of you?" Dawson snaps.

"It seems that two years ago, they all were separated, but all of them have been re-united as of the beginning of this school year," states Miss. Brooks.

"What?" Dawson asks.

"Yes, sir. The parents of all of the children who have shown these reading level increases are all recently reunited," Miss. Brooks clarifies.

"Are you serious?" Dawson asks.

"Very," Miss. Andrews confirms. "And that's not the half of it. The fathers that we spoke to all said that they made the decision to get their families back together after meeting and talking with a man whom they say called himself Arwis."

"Arwis?" Dawson repeats the name.

"Arwis," Miss. Andrews confirms.

"How could one man convince so many men to return to a family that they had left?" Dawson questions them.

"That we don't know yet, but we don't think that he has stopped. We think that we are going to see much more of this," Miss. Daniels clarifies.

Still unable to believe what he is being told, Dawson states, "This is not making sense. What you're suggesting is impossible! How could one man—?

"Impossible though it may seem it is happening, and if you ask me, I think it's great," Miss. Daniels interrupts. "These test scores are real. These children have been affected in a positive way. I really think it's great. And I hope this is not the end of it. Two of these men said that they were about to end their marriages but changed their minds after talking with Arwis."

"How is this Arwis person selecting these men? How does he know that they are estranged or having family problems?" Dawson questions them.

"We don't know that, sir," says Miss. Andrews. "Hopefully, he will be willing to tell us that when we have a chance to talk with him, but so far, we have not been able to."

"Don't any of these men know how to contact him?" asks Dawson.

Replying to him, Miss. Andrews states, "We believe that they do, but they are reluctant to tell us where to find him. They don't feel that it is necessary for us to talk to him."

"I want all of these men interviewed again. We need to talk to this Arwis person," orders Dawson. "Lina, schedule a hearing and invite them all to attend. We need to get to the bottom of this."

"Yes, sir. For what date shall I schedule the hearing?" Lina confirms with Dawson.

Taking his palm pilot out of his inside pocket, Dawson begins to check his calendar. "One week from today, 10 am," he states.

"One day will not be enough time to interview all of them, sir," Lina puts in objectively.

"Yes, well, schedule hearings for the entire week," Dawson replies.

"But sir—" Lina tries to object.

"No buts, this is very serious. It must take priority. Reschedule everything else." Dawson states firmly.

"Yes, sir."

All look at each other as Dawson and Lina leave the room.

***

A week later, the Board of Education's hearing room is filled with black men of ages ranging from 18 to 50. They are in various modes of dress and wearing the family symbol pin on their collars, lapels, ties, hats, etc. Some official mumbo jumbo is heard, and then the clerk calls a man to be sworn in.

"Will Mr. Phillip Carter please come forward to be interviewed?"

A casually dressed man, about 30, approaches the front of the room, is sworn in, and is seated.

"Mr. Carter, do you know why you are here?" asks Dawson.

"Yes, you want to learn more about Arwis and about our children's progress over the last seven months," replies Mr. Carter.

"That's right, Mr. Carter. You will admit that it is not every day that this kind of thing happens," states Dawson. "Will you tell us about it?"

"Well, we think that it will be happening every day from now on. You see, we think that Arwis is our guardian angel," replies Mr. Carter.

"An angel? And just why do you think that? Did he tell you that he was an angel? asks Dawson.

"Well, no, not exactly," Mr. Carter replies.

"Then why do you think he is an angel?" Dawson questions him.

"Well, this is going to sound strange to you, but when I first met him, it was in a dream. As a matter of fact, I met Arwis and nineteen of the men present in this dream," states Mr. Carter.

Dawson sits upright, raises one eyebrow, and gives Mr. Carter a look as if sizing him up for a straitjacket. He looks left and right at the panel members, leans way back in his chair, folds his arms, and says, "Please continue, Mr. Carter."

"It was eight months ago, on my son's birthday. The other nineteen men have sons who have birthdays in the first week of July also. Arwis told us that all of our sons wished for their parents to be back together when they blew out the candles on their birthday cakes. In the dream, Arwis explained to us how the broken family syndrome had almost caused his life to be prematurely ended like it has done for thousands of other children, and that's how he came to be on the mission to start the "Family Restoration Movement." Mr. Carter revealed.

"Come now, Mr. Carter, do you expect us to believe that you met Arwis and nineteen of these men in a dream?" asks Dawson skeptically.

"You can believe what you will, sir. You asked me to tell you how I met him. Well, as incredible as it sounds, that's how it happened," Mr. Carter replies.

Several of the men mumble affirmations while shaking their heads. Dawson looks left to right at the panel members and says, "Please continue, Mr. Carter."

"Arwis told us that he was here to give us another chance to save ourselves and our families," explains Mr. Carter. "In the dream, we were all sitting on the grass near the band shell in Flushing Meadows Park. Arwis asked us if we had any idea of how big the mistake was that we were making. At first, there was a lot of resistance and disagreement. Some of us didn't think it was such a big deal not being around to raise our children. Many of us, in fact, most of us, were not raised in two-parent households. We only had our mothers. We loved our mothers, hated our fathers, whom we seldom or never saw, and we didn't see our children's situations as being much worse than our own had been."

"Arwis taught us different," Mr. Carter states. "He told us that no matter what we thought to the contrary, the worst thing that we could ever do would be to leave our families in a broken state. He stressed that we should not hate our fathers for not being there for us because we didn't really know what issues they were faced with during their time. He said, 'Hate what they did or didn't do; hate what they were about or involved themselves in, but don't hate them.' He said that we were them and that hating them would create a kind of bio-feedback that would cause us to hate ourselves and not know it."

"He took us all on a spiritual and emotional journey, and we are all glad that he did," Mr. Carter continues as he recalls the day at Forest Park where a band shell had been set up. He remembers the strange reddish hue in the sky as Arwis talks to twenty men who range in age from 18 to about 30. Their attire ranges from well-dressed to shabbily dressed. Some look angry, some perplexed, and others have a blank expression. The band shell in the background is set up as if for a concert.

Arwis says, "I know that you all want to know why you are here. Well, you all have something in common. You all have families that, for one reason or another, you chose to leave. You have all been affected by things that happened to your ancestors hundreds of years ago that are still impacting your lives and behavior today. From Willie Lynch in 1712 right up till today. Lynch's method was exactly that of Alexander the Great. "Divide and Conquer." This strategy of making us slaves and keeping us divided, separated, apart from and opposed to each other has been and is still effective."

As Arwis speaks, he describes several incidents of injustice that have been done. He talks about slave families being sold and separated, blacks being beaten for reading, smiling politicians making speeches, and white guards and black prisoners. He also narrates to the group an incident about a child looking sheepish after being brought to school by a truant officer and the dialogue with the parents about him getting caught playing hooky.

"Go get me a switch."

The child, teary-eyed, replies, "Yes, ma'am."

Arwis continues his discussion with the group about the stark differences in their lives and shares an example of a group of happy kids going to the swimming pool while a smaller group of sad children are headed for summer school. "We have graduates who are having trouble reading a document at graduation, getting rejected for jobs, or selling drugs on the corner. There are young people watching music videos of young girls being sexually exploited, fancy cars, houses, and clothes, young folks being arrested, and young mothers and children looking on," he adds.

"Our people are still under-educated, under-employed, unfairly represented in politics, and tricked into believing in leaders who sell us out and exploit us for the sake of making life better for themselves. Nowadays, private institutions have become big businesses providing jobs for thousands of people, a few of which are people of color. In order to run prisons, there must be a population of prisoners. Black people make up the largest percentage of prisoners in the country and are being systematically herded into these prisons. A close look at certain policies makes it plain to see. Let me explain. There used to be someone called the truant officer who would patrol the neighborhoods during school hours and apprehend all school-aged children who were found in the streets during school hours and take them either to their homes or to their schools. Knowing that these officers were out patrolling the streets for truants served to deter many children from hooking school. In those days, children had reverence for their parents, their teachers, and their adult neighbors. When an adult spoke to you, you responded with respect. You said, 'Yes, sir,' or 'Yes, ma'am.' You knew that if word got back to your parents of your behaving badly in school or in the streets, you were in big trouble, but you knew that you were loved."

Arwis continues, "Most of the time, you knew that the behind beatings that you got, you deserved. Remember "getting left back?" It meant summer school. Parents' wrath, summer school, and embarrassment served to encourage students to get promoted. Religious instruction and prayer in school helped to give children a sense of right thinking and good behavior. There were far fewer incidents of violence in school before these were taken out, and on Sunday, with no ifs, ands, or buts about it, you went to church. We had a veneration of our parents, our God, our teachers, and adults in general, not like today. No, no, today, children are allowed to hook school and walk the streets as much as they please. If they don't make the grade, they are promoted anyway. There is no religious instruction in many schools, and teachers, neighbors, concerned adults, and even parents are not allowed to punish children without being chided or, even worse, being charged with child abuse. Today, children of color are promoted right out of school without the ability to read the diplomas that they are given. They are now young adults who don't have academic skills sufficient to get a decent job, and so thousands of them turn to selling drugs and/or stealing to get by, which lands them in prison. Some find it impossible to get legal work and equally impossible to avoid illegal opportunities. Other factors that help with the breeding of prisoners are the media, the music, and the video industry. These glamorized lifestyles influence young people of color to pursue unattainable, unrealistic, unsavory, unhealthy, and unsafe goals, such as flamboyant lifestyles, fancy cars, flashy clothes,

17

expensive jewelry, drug and alcohol use and abuse, and premature and unsafe sex. The content of much of today's music and videos promotes domestic violence and disrespect for family, friends, women, the law, God, and self. The result is that thousands more of our children, especially those with no fathers, find themselves as fodder for the prison system. Like so many others across this country, you are suffering from post-Willie Lynch Syndrome. How many of you have heard of Willie Lynch?"

Arwis pauses, and four men raise their hands. Arwis, looking at the men, says, "I want all of you to go on to the internet and find the "Willie Lynch Speech," read it, understand it, and pass it on to every black person that you know. It's time for a change. You men have been chosen to be the first movementors of the "Family Restoration Movement." Through being involved with the Movement, it will become clear to you just how important each stable family is to the success of our race. A lot of money is being spent to keep our people on the bottom rung of the social ladder. Many of us are also unwittingly helping in this effort. For example, we still use the dreaded N----- word. Later, we will deal with this in depth. In the meantime, resign yourselves to stop using it."

The men mumble.

"We must restore our families, keep them intact, and make them prosper. We black men must take the necessary steps to make this happen. We will, to borrow a phrase,

"Endeavor to Persevere." It won't be easy, but it will be right, and know this: being involved with the "Family Restoration Movement" will help us to break the chains that bind our minds, help us to think in terms of 'we,' 'us,' 'our,' instead of 'me,' 'my,' and 'I;' help us to better understand the power of the "collective love," and stop being lethargic about it. We all know that we have had enough of oppression, hatred, prejudice, racism, crime, war, domestic violence, drug addiction, religious confusion and "what ain't right." We never deserved to be treated like this. We owe it to ourselves and our families to change things. True, the white man did us wrong, but he doesn't owe us as much as we owe us. I suggest that we pay up. Forget about reparations for now. Focus on the Movement; Fate pays credit where credit is due," Arwis adds as the group applauds.

Continuing, he states, "The late Dr. Martin Luther King Jr. sang, 'We shall overcome someday.' I tell you that for you, that someday is today," he says as more applause follows.
"How many of you remember the song, *Our Day Will Come*?" Arwis pauses and sees all hands go up.

"Well, I'm here to tell you that our day HAS come. The Family Restoration Movement will help us as a people to learn and share a most important and valuable lesson. It is the only lesson in the Christian bible, or in any other bible for that matter, the lesson of "unselfish love." Do you realize that man's selfishness is the only reason that homelessness, hunger, poverty, alcoholism, drug addiction, illiteracy, and a number of other social ills still exist?"

As the group mumbles, Arwis continues, "In a short time, you will find that operating in the "collective love" will allow us to accomplish all of our goals, but the first step towards developing this race-wide, "collective love" begins with and in each individual black family, but the "collective love" can't operate for you and your family if you are not with your family. You brothers are not here by accident. You were chosen. The collective wish of your children brought you here. You have been given another chance to make it happen for your families. Don't throw it away again."

Keith Hazelwood, a strapping out-of-work construction worker, stands up and says, "It's all well and good to say that we want to make our families successful. Many of us know that we need to and want to be with our families, but many of us, myself included, have no jobs, no education, and no money. These are some of the reasons that many of our families have failed in the first place."

The group mumbles affirmations, and grumbles are heard.

Donald Parks, who lost his job when his company decided to move its operation to CA and could have moved with it, but his wife was not willing to give up her job and move, says, "He's right; many of our women are dissatisfied. As a matter of fact, my woman put me out after I lost my job. I had no control over my company moving away."

Michael Brooks, who had also lost his job when his company left the city, chimes in, saying, "Same thing happened to me. The marriage vows say "for better or for worse," but my wife was only concerned with the better. I never thought that she would turn on me the way she did. I was doing my best. I know several brothers whose women have. I hate to say it, but it's like they have turned white on us." More mumbles and grumbles are heard from the group, and he continues, "Some of us had to get away from our women to preserve our sanity and, in many cases, our freedom. Hassling and fighting with our women have caused many brothers to wind up in jail. Like the brother said, many of us have no skills, no education, and no job. Some of us are even homeless. How are we gonna go back to our families? We have to solve these problems first."

Arwis says, "You're right, guys, you're absolutely right. In the words of one of our greatest leaders, Malcolm X, 'We must think first, then act with intelligence.' He also said, 'A nation cannot rise that degrades its women.' Our women have been tricked, bamboozled, hoodwinked, run amuck, led astray, and made to be ungrateful and unappreciative of black men."

Michael responds, "Elevating black women above black men is another strategy that sometimes leads to the breakup of relationships and families."

21

Arwis adds to it, saying, "True, but we have many strong and dedicated black women, women who would stick with their men through thick and thin, but the real culprit is male macho, male pride, male ignorance, and male ego that leads to the actual breakup of the family. Believe this, being involved with the "Family Restoration Movement" will help us to solve and correct the problems that our families are facing. The Movement has established Family Promoters Incorporated (FPI). This company is to be owned and operated by you, the members of the Movement. You have talent, skills, and abilities that have heretofore been exploited by the system. FPI is going to change all of that. This company was formed for the purpose of providing jobs, counseling, and security to all who would join the Movement."

Arwis pauses as more applause follows before continuing, "You are going to have jobs, and your needs are going to be met. We have created many problems for ourselves in the past and the present by allowing ourselves to be tricked into focusing on our wants more so than on our needs, which ultimately makes us fall short of both. You will come to understand that once your needs are met, your wants will not be so difficult to obtain. Oftentimes, you will discover that they are one and the same. This will undoubtedly serve to ease much stress and tension in your minds and relationships. One of our most important needs is to have our children educated. We must all come to recognize our own need for continued learning. Learning is earning your knowledge. If you continue your learning, you will be more able to see to it that your children get educated. Your children are your contribution to this world, your contribution to the universe. You made them. They are you. They are your future. It is on you to see to it that they are educated. *GET IT DONE.* You will have the Movement, all of its movementaries, FPI, and the power of the "collective love" to help you, but you must *GET IT DONE.*"

The men are silent, hearing Arwis' impassioned speech.

Chapter 2 - Where's Daddy?

The men are silent, thinking as Arwis continues to talk. "In the Movement, men will no longer create a family and then walk off and leave them to fend for themselves. Too many of these children grow up to be uneducated, unproductive, and undesirables who turn to crime for survival and wind up in prison. There are too many fathers and not enough Daddies. Any fool with a penis can be a father, but it takes a real man to face up to his responsibilities and be a daddy. Fathers make babies; daddies raise children. A real man treats his wife with love, kindness, understanding, and respect. He doesn't beat on her or cheat on her. He protects her. Ideally, he marries her, creates a stable, loving family environment, and raises his children in it. A father, mother, and children equals a family, whether married or not. Statistics show that not all but most children who grow up in one-parent families tend to become less than what their potential is. This is unfair to the children. They don't ask to be born, and they do have a right to be treated fairly. Too many of them don't have the opportunity to have a meaningful relationship with their fathers. Many never find out who their fathers are, which tends to have a negative effect on them for the whole of their lives. We must change this. Family begins with the father."

Charles Frazier, a driver for Coca-Cola with a seven-year-old son, is sitting near the back of the group. He recently left his wife and felt that it was her fault. He says, "It takes two to make a baby, though, right?"

Arwis responds, "That's true. It does take two to make a baby, but the father makes it happen."

Charles, unable to hold his views back, says, "You just said it takes two. Why are women not equally responsible for starting a family?"

Arwis says, "Let me ask you a question. How is the embryo formed?"

"The male sperm and the female egg join and form the embryo. It's still 50/50," Charles responds.

"Do female egg cells leave their place of origin?" Arwis asks.

Charles answers, "Only if they are not fertilized, then they pass out as waste."

"Right, now think about the male sperm cells," Arwis retorts.

Charles ponders for a few seconds, then says, "I see what you mean, Arwis; sperm cells do leave their place of origin and go into the woman to seek out, penetrate, and fertilize an egg."

Arwis questions again, "And when this is accomplished?"

Shaking his head in the affirmative, Charles speaks, "It is the beginning of a new natural nuclear family. Now I understand where you were coming from. Family does begin with Father. I never looked at it like that before. This is something that I should have learned from my father."

Arwis, still not done schooling him, says, "And who should your son learn it from?"

Charles is silent for a moment, looking down at the floor. He raises his head, looks at Arwis, and walks to him. They hug, and Arwis turns back to address the group.

"Let me tell you all a little story," he says. "There was a man who owned a pit bulldog that he said was a vicious dog by nature. To heighten the dog's viciousness, the owner would antagonize the animal by beating it, feeding it hot sauce, and exploding firecrackers near him. The owner knew full well that the animal was very dangerous and that anyone who got too close to the animal would face serious danger. One day, the owner set the dog on an unsuspecting person. As you would expect, the dog attacked and mauled the person severely. When the police came and raised the question of who is at fault, the only truthful answer was that the owner was responsible for what the dog did to the person because he, the owner, knew what the dog would do before he set him on the person."

Looking around the group, he continues, "Now I want to compare sperm cells to a pit bull. Sperm cells have an agenda. They do one thing. They seek out female eggs to fertilize and make babies. The owner of the sperm cells knows exactly what they will do if unleashed. Sending sperm cells on their journey requires effort. The owner has to engage in some activity to work the cells up and propel them on their journey. When the sperm cells are ejaculated, as you would expect, they do what they are designed to do. They seek out an egg, fertilize it, and make a baby. There is only one answer to the question, 'Who is responsible for the baby?' The owner of the sperm cell, of course, because he knew what the result of his actions would be. RESPONSIBILITY!"

For a long moment, there is silence, and then Keith Hazelwood speaks. "I think I speak for all of us here when I say that we are feeling you now, Arwis. Our question is, where do we go from here? How do we establish ourselves in the Family Restoration Movement?"

Arwis picks up a briefcase, sets it on his lap, and opens it. He removes a black velvet tray with twenty golden Family

Symbol pins on it. He hands the tray to Danny Delaine, a handsome twenty-five-year-old songwriter who is sitting in the front of the group and closest to him. Danny removes a pin from the tray, passes it to Nick Matthews, a twenty-one-year-old former drug dealer seated next to him, and then begins to attach his pin to the front of his cap.

Arwis then stands and points to the pin on the left lapel of his suit jacket, saying, "This is the Family Symbol Pin." He pauses for a moment, then says again, "This pin will identify you as Movementors. In two days, we will meet at FPI to establish jobs, training, and positions for all of you. There is great work to be done. This symbol will be the emblem on the flag that represents the nation of family. All of us, by virtue of our birth, are royal subjects in the nation of family. The pledge of allegiance to the nation and flag of a family is "**F**ather **A**nd **M**other, **I L**ove **Y**ou." The '**I**' in the pledge represents each and every one of us. Let us all together pledge our allegiance to the nation of family and to the Family Restoration Movement by reciting the pledge together."

The group recites the pledge, "**F**ather **A**nd **M**other, **I Love Y**ou." They applaud themselves, shake hands, and hug each other.

***

Mr. Carter concludes recounting his meeting with Arwis to Dawson, saying, "That's how I met Arwis. Two days later, we received letters that instructed us to come to FPI for interviews, job placements, training assignments, and assignments to various positions in the company. FPI assisted some of us in obtaining housing, medical treatment, and emergency monies. We contacted our wives and re-established our families and relationships. We are all doing well. Our children are doing well, and we are identifying others who have the same need that we had to save their families and are encouraging them to join the movement."

As Mr. Carter stops narrating the incident, the panel seems to be mesmerized. The room is so quiet that you can hear a pin drop in the room. Dawson shakes his head as if to wake himself from a trance and says, "That was an absolutely incredible story, Mr. Carter. Really incredible! Could you…uh… Could you tell us where FPI is located?"

"The address is 5410 Halsey St, in downtown Brooklyn," Mr. Carter says.

"Can Arwis be reached at this location?" Dawson asks.

"Sometimes," replies Mr. Carter.

"Is he there now?" Dawson asks.

"I don't know, sir. As you know, I've been here all morning," Mr. Carter replies.

"Right! Forgive me, Mr. Carter. Could you give the phone number to FPI to the clerk?" Dawson requests.

Mr. Carter removes a card from his inside pocket and hands it to the clerk, saying, "This card has all of the information on it."

"Thank you, Mr. Carter; we appreciate your cooperation. You may step down."

The commissioner puts his hand over his microphone and leans over to converse privately with a few members of the panel.

"Could we have a show of hands of those of you who were not present at this dream meeting with Arwis?" Dawson asks.

All the men not present in the dream meeting raise their hands. Pointing to one of the men, Dawson says, "You, sir. Would you come forward to be interviewed?" A casually dressed man comes forward, about thirty, wearing the family symbol pin on the right lapel of his shirt collar.

"Would you state your name, please?" the clerk requests.

The man replies, "My name is Kenneth Evans."

The clerk says, "Please be seated, Mr. Evans."

Dawson says, "Mr. Evans, would you tell us how and under what circumstances you came to know the man known as Arwis?"

One of the panel members leans over and whispers something in the commissioner's ear. Dawson says, "Oh yes, and would you tell us if you also think that Arwis is an angel?"

Smiling, Mr. Evans replies, "Yes, sir, I guess I do. No, I don't guess I do; I do. Okay. Where to begin? Well, I've been married for almost nine years now. About a year and a half ago, my wife and I started having serious problems in our marriage. We began to fight over just about everything. She, my wife, began to complain constantly about all of the things that we didn't have. She wanted a better car, a larger apartment, and better furniture; she was upset because we couldn't afford to go on vacations like her sisters and her friends did. She began accusing me of being with other women. I mean everything. She was driving me crazy. We argued so much till I began to dread coming home. One night, I had worked late, and when I got home…" he trails off as he narrates the incident.

***

Mr. Evans arrives home late from work. Karen Evans, 5'5", a very attractive woman with a wrap hairstyle and a drop-dead figure, is coming down the hall toward him, wearing a short-sleeved white blouse and jeans.

Karen says, "Did you get the increase?"

Mr. Evans hangs his coat on the hall coat rack, not answering her.

"Did you even ask about the raise, Ken? You didn't, did you?" Karen snaps.

"Karen, could you let me get in the house before you start?" Mr. Evans replies, irritated.

Karen, undeterred, says, "You promised that you would ask about the increase today. Well, did you?"

"Where's Junior?" Mr. Evans asks, ignoring her question entirely.

"He's in bed. Where do you think he is? Did you ask about the raise or not?" Karen repeats the question.

"Yes, Karen, I did," Mr. Evans finally says.

Mr. Evans finishes hanging up his coat, walks down the hall, and looks in on his son, who appears to be asleep. He then comes back to the living room, where Karen is still standing by the door. He enters the living room, a large, bright room with a three-piece L-shaped sectional couch that extends the length of one wall and turns along another. A large mirror hangs over the couch, and a recliner chair sits caddy-cornered a short distance from the short end of the couch. White-laced curtains hang behind the short side of the couch and extend across the wall behind the recliner. A black Formica entertainment center with a large screen TV in its center is opposite the long couch on the opposite wall. A few feet away is a computer desk with a flat-screen computer that has been left on. Above the computer desk is a large black velvet picture of a beautiful, shapely black woman lying on the beach. One wall is covered with a collage of family pictures. A four-foot-long glass-topped coffee table sits in the middle of the room.

As Mr. Evans enters the living room, his wife is right behind him. Anxious, she asks, "Well, what did he say?"

Mr. Evans, clearly annoyed, replies, "He said that he couldn't do it now, maybe in a couple of months. Things are kind of slow right now."

Aggravated, Karen says, "Things are kind of slow! He's been saying things are slow for the last six months."

Mr. Evans turns the computer off, walks over, and picks up the remote, flopping down on the couch and turning on the TV.

Clearly agitated, he says, "Karen, please; business is slow. Since 9/11, I'm lucky to get the overtime that I get. It's not the end of the world, and we're doing alright."

Karen walks over to the computer desk and picked up a stack of envelopes. She walks over to her husband and throws the stack down on the table before him.

"Alright? Alright? You call this doing alright? You know the car insurance went up after that accident, and the credit card bills are piling up. And you promised we'd get new living room furniture, and I want to get Junior's braces and—"

"Karen, PLEASE!" Mr. Evans shouts. "I'm doing my best. What more do you want? I can't force them to give me a raise, and you know that that accident wasn't my fault, and there's nothing wrong with this furniture, and Junior's braces will just have to wait. If you let your mother live with your sister for a while, we could save some money. She's always on the phone, running up the bill. She's always spending money on booze and, lotto tickets and bingo. Not to mention, she's always in our business."

Karen moves to a spot where she is between her husband and the TV. She puts her left hand on her hip, points her finger at him while gyrating her neck, and says, "Don't start on my mother again. You know she doesn't want to move down south because all of her friends are here..."

Mr. Evans leans over to try to see around her and gestures with his hand, saying, "Move, Karen, you're blocking the TV. Could you fix me some dinner and stop fussing?"

"...And you know she doesn't get along with Donald anyway, so don't even go there. And she helps me with Junior and..." Karen continues on.

The voice on the television announces that there was a single winner of the $ 115,000,000 lottery and that the winner wishes to accept the lump sum payout but wishes to remain anonymous.

"Karen, you are bugging me out. Nothing I do is good enough for you," Mr. Evans says. He picks up the remote and starts surfing channels. The phone rings. Karen walks over and answers it.

Karen says, "Hello. Hello?"

No one answers; she hears them hang up, and she slams the phone down, walking across the room and sitting in her favorite spot: the recliner by the window.

"That was probably that Hussy. Are you sure you were putting in overtime or other time? I know that's who that was," Karen says.

"Don't start that again, Karen. It was probably just a wrong number," Mr. Evans remarks.

"Yeah, right. I'll bet it was that doggone—"

Before she can finish, Mr. Evans interrupts, saying, "I can't take much more of this, Karen. Why don't you just chill out and fix me something to eat like I asked you to? "

"Oh, now you can't take much more? What are you gonna do? Leave?" Karen says curtly.

"I'm warning you, Karen, don't tempt me. You know you don't want me to leave you," Mr. Evans warns.

Karen's mother, Helen Cooper, an attractive middle-aged woman, prematurely gray for her age, sticks her head in the door, holding a wine cooler in one hand and a piece of sausage in the other, and says, "You all need to stop that arguing before you wake up, Junior."

She immediately goes back to her room and closes the door.

Karen resumes her verbal assault on Mr. Evans, saying, "Don't flatter yourself, Ken. I could do just as well on welfare. You're never home anyway, and you're always too tired when I ask you to take me out somewhere; no, you never want to take me out, but you're never too tired to hang out with your friends."

"I put in three hours overtime tonight, and I am tired. When I come, instead of you greeting me with a kiss or a 'how was your day,' the first thing out of your mouth is, 'Did you ask for the raise?' You're really pissing me off, you know. Just leave me alone, Karen. I'm tired of listening to your foolishness!" retorts Mr. Evans.

"So what? You going to leave now?" Karen replies sarcastically.

"Why do you keep talking about me leaving? Is that what you want, Karen? Do you really want me to leave? If you keep this up, I will leave," Mr. Evans replies.

Now shouting, Karen says, "WELL, LEAVE THEN. GO AHEAD AND LEAVE. You probably want to leave anyway, so leave. Good riddance!"

Mr. Evans gets up and heads for his bedroom. He picks up a suitcase, puts it on the bed, and starts throwing things into it.

Junior, eight years old, is in his bedroom and has been sitting by the slightly opened door listening to the argument. He gets up, throws himself on his bed, and starts to cry.
***

Chapter 3 - East or West

The aura in the hearing room is a bit tense.

"I didn't really want to leave my family, but I was about to bug out. I really couldn't take it anymore. I was doing my best, but she just wasn't satisfied. So, I left. I went to stay with a friend in CA. He's in the music business and went on a tour, so I stayed in his apartment. I got a job in a restaurant in Beverly Hills and was doing okay. I thought about my family a lot, and I also thought about going back, but every time I called home, we argued. One day, about six months after I had left, I was at work…" Mr. Evans tells Dawson.

***

It is a luncheonette-type restaurant with six booths along one wall, an area with six tables, and a twelve-foot lunch counter. There are several customers seated at tables, two young boys at the counter, and Mr. Evans behind the counter.

Evans thinks, *wow, that kid looks just like Junior. I wonder how old he is. He's probably the same age as my Jr.*

Oblivious to Evans, who is in deep thought, a man comes in and sits two stools away from the boys. Evans is snapped out of his trance with his boss's voice.

His boss shouts, "Evans, snap out of your daze; you have another customer."

Evans, shaking his head, says, "Oh, sorry, I was…"

Arwis, the mysterious stranger, seemingly an ethereal being, materializes in moments of dire need, offering solace and aid, especially to those from 'dysfunctional' or broken families. Cloaked in mystery, he possesses an aura of compassion and wisdom that transcends the mortal realm. With gentle words and profound insights, he imparts guidance and uplifts weary souls, kindling hope within their hearts.

However, as abruptly as he appeared, the strange man appears to dissolve into the fabric of the unknown, leaving behind a profound impact, a whispered reminder of the power of his angelic presence and the transformative nature of his interventions.

Arwis says, "Thinking of your son?"

Evans, looking amazed, says, "How did you know that? Do I know you? I mean, do you know me? I mean, how did you know that I was thinking of my son? How did you know that?"

"Could I have a cup of hot chocolate and a toasted corn muffin, please?" Arwis says.

Looking perplexed, Evans fixes the chocolate, thinking, *How the hell did he know what I was thinking? Who is that guy?"*

"No, no, Kareem, the sun does not rise in the west and set in the east; it rises in the east and sets in the west," the first boy at the counter says.

The first boy is sitting two stools down on Arwis' right, while the second boy is next to him on the first's right.

The first boy turns to Arwis and says, "Isn't that right, mister?"

Arwis, looking at the boy, says, "That's right, son, for *you*, the sun rises in the east and sets in the west."

The boy says, "See, I told you, Kareem."

The boys pay for their sodas and leave.

37

Evans, looking quite perplexed, is pondering Arwis' answer. "Excuse me! Why did you tell that boy that, for him, the sun rises in the east? Doesn't it rise in the east for everyone?" Evans asks.

Arwis says, "For him, the sun does rise in the east, but for you, Kenneth Evans, son rises in the father."

Evans says, "How do you know my name? Do you know me? I mean, do I know you?"

"You said that before," Arwis retorts.

Evans says, "Well, do you? Ugh… I mean, do I? Look, who are you?"

Arwis hands him an envelope and says, "My name is Arwis. Take this and go home."

"What is this?" Evans asks.

Arwis says, "It's a gift to cover the patent fee for your multi-colored stamp pad invention. Take it and go home. Your family needs you. Your son deserves the right to be the I. He's not doing well in school. He wished for you to be home. Go home. Don't you love your family?"

Surprised and frowning, Evans says, "How did you know about my stamp pad invention? And what do you mean he has the right to be the I? And what do you know about my family…? Who are you?"

Arwis says, "I told you; my name is Arwis."

"Excuse me," someone at the counter says, and Evans turns to see an elderly lady.

"May I have some service over here, please?" she asks.

"Just one second, ma'am," Evans says. When he turns back, Arwis is gone. Evans looks around, completely puzzled.

***

Mr. Evans says as he continues narrating the story in the hearing room, "Yes, I do think he's an angel. All that day in my mind, I could hear over and over Arwis saying, 'The son rises in the father' And 'Go home; your family needs you.' *The son rises in the father. Go home; your family needs you*, it kept repeating in my mind. I wondered how he disappeared like that and why. Yes, I think he could be an angel. That night, I decided to go back home to my family, and I got there just short of too late."

***

The dark of the night has taken over, and Evans is in his street. As Evans approaches his building, he sees smoke coming out of the windows. He rushes in to find his wife has fallen asleep with a cigarette that set the curtains on fire. He pulls her out into the hallway and goes back into his son's room. He gathers him up in a blanket, takes him outside to Karen, and then goes back into his mother-in-law's room. He can hear the sirens in the distance. He comes back out.

"Karen, where is your mother?" Evans asks.

Karen, crying and coughing, says, "She went to stay the night with Miss Ida."

Firemen rushed in and started putting out the fire. A crowd had gathered by now.

Evans, hugging his wife and son, says, "I love you, Karen. I'm sorry; everything is going to be alright now."

Evans does a double take as, for a split second, he thinks he is seeing Arwis in the crowd.

***

In the hearing room with Dawson, Mr. Evans says, "Like I said, I got home just short of too late to save my family. That night, we went to stay with my brother. A couple of days later, I got a call from Arwis, who told me to come to FPI. I went. They helped me to secure the patent for my invention, the first ever multi-color stamp pad. We marketed it, and the sales have been very good. Now, I work for FPI as a product developer. My son is doing much better in school. My family is doing fine. I'm a family restoration movementor."

Again, the room is quiet for a long moment, then Dawson says, "Thank you, Mr. Evans. You may step down. We will break for lunch for one hour. We will resume the interviews at 1:00 p.m. sharp," Dawson announces.

***

Once the break is over, the commissioner and five of his panel are once again seated at one table in the cafeteria.

Miss Brooks says, "Sir, you didn't ask about what was done to cause their children's reading levels to go up so drastically. Surely, you don't think that just the fact that their parents got back together caused it, do you?"

Dawson replies, "No, I didn't, and no, I don't. I was enthralled by the stories of their encounters with this Arwis person. As for the cause of the sudden academic acceleration in these children, it is true that the trauma of parents divorcing has been known to have devastatingly negative effects on some children, causing them to lose interest in many things and to lower their performance levels in a number of areas. It might well be true that the mere re-uniting of their parents could have just the opposite effect in a few cases, but definitely not in 94 cases - of that, I am sure. I'm convinced that there is more to it than that. We simply have to know just exactly what is happening to these children to cause this. Do you understand what this could mean? Do you realize what they could..."

He has a strained look on his face as if he is afraid of something. He actually seems a bit nervous. He makes eye contact with Ms. Clark and suddenly stops mid-sentence, changing his subject.

Ms. Clark says, "They could what, sir?"

"Those were two rather amazing stories, weren't they? I mean, an angel. Do any of you believe that this Arwis person could be a real angel?" Dawson asks.

Ms. Clark does not push for an answer to her question, but she does raise one eyebrow and gives him a curious look.

Miss Daniels says, "Well, during the hearings, I looked it up, and Webster's second meaning describes an angel as a guiding spirit or influence, and in light of what is happening, Arwis could certainly be considered an angel in that respect. That could be what they meant. Shouldn't we call FPI and speak to him?"

Dawson replies, "Yes, do it. Try to set up an appointment with him."

Miss Daniels takes out her cell phone and places the call.

The voice on the phone says, "Family Promoters Incorporated; Carmen Smith speaking. How may I direct your call?"

Miss Daniels replies, "Hello, this is Miss Daniels at the Board of Education. I am calling to arrange a meeting for Commissioner Dawson to speak with Mr. Arwis. May I speak with him, please?"

Ms. Smith says, "One moment, please."

Miss Daniels, covering the phone with one hand, says to Dawson, "I've been put on hold."

Dawson says, "Ask if he can meet with me today."

Ms. Smith gets back on call and says, "I'm sorry, Miss Daniels, Arwis is out of town today. Would you like to leave a message for him?"

Miss Daniels says, "Yes, please inform him that Commissioner Dawson would appreciate an audience with him at his earliest convenience.

M. Smith responds, "I'm expecting him to call in. When he does, I will give him your message, and I'm sure he will get back to you. Blessings on your family, goodbye."

Miss Daniels beams a warm smile, saying, "Thank you." She then turns to Dawson and says, "He's out of town today, sir. I spoke to Ms. Smith. She said that she is expecting him to call in for messages."

Dawson says, "Why are you smiling?"

"Before she hung up, she said, 'Blessings on your family.' I've never heard that on the telephone before. I thought that was very nice. I mean, that's like wishing the gift of happiness or favor to my family. I really love my family, and I think that is a very nice telephone closing for a company to have," Miss Daniels says.

Ms. Clark says, "I would like to know more about the significance of that pin that they all wear."

Dawson replies, "Make a note to ask about it during the next testimony. I will also ask if they did anything specific to help to increase their children's reading levels. Another thing that we need to know is..."

***

Back in the hearing room, the clerk says, "Will Mr. Bill Collins, please come forward to give testimony?"

A six-foot-one-inch, 35-year-old man comes forward and makes himself comfortable in the interviewee's chair.

Dawson says, "Mr. Collins, as you know, these hearings are being conducted to help us gather information as to the cause of what we are calling academic acceleration in your children. Not only have all of their reading scores improved significantly in a short time, but several of the children have shown marked improvement in other areas as well, such as sports, art, and music."

Mr. Collins says, "Yes, sir, and we are very proud and pleased with those improvements."

Dawson replies, "Also, Mr. Collins, we understand that many of you are involved in a "Family Restoration Movement," which is something that we have just recently become aware of, and we would like to know more about that and its leader, Mr. Arwis."

"First, let me say that he prefers to be called simply Arwis. Also, I must correct you on another point. Arwis is not the leader of the Family Restoration Movement. According to him, he merely started it for us. We, the Movementors, are all leaders. You see, according to the Movement, Family Restoration begins with the Father, and since we are all Fathers, that makes us all leaders of the Movement to Restore our Families. Get it?" Mr. Collins replies.

Dawson, scratching his head with a puzzled look on his face, says, "Umm… Okay, Mr. Collins, could you please tell us how you came to meet Arwis, what caused you to decide to restore your family, and if you think that is what affected your child's improvement?"

Mr. Collins says, "This is going to take a few minutes."

"That's quite alright, Mr. Collins. Take your time," Dawson says.

"Well, about a year ago, I was returning from a basketball tournament in North Carolina. I was at the airport getting my bags checked in, and Arwis was in line behind me. There was an announcement that our flight would be delayed for half an hour, and we struck up a conversation about it," says Mr. Collins as he begins to narrate his meeting with Arwis.
***

At the NC International Airport, Mr. Collins is standing at the ticket counter; Arwis is four feet behind him in the waiting line, followed by six people in the queue.

"Attention passengers for flight 717 to New York City, JFK Airport. There will be a thirty-minute delay of departure," comes the announcement over the PA system.

Mr. Collins turns and faces Arwis, his palms facing the ceiling. He shrugs his shoulders and says, Do you believe this? This happened when I was coming down here. That flight was delayed for two hours."

Arwis says, "I prefer a weather delay to a high jacking delay. I heard that there was a box cutter found on one of the earlier flights, and it was delayed for hours, too."

Mr. Collins says, "Is that right? Alright, Osama, don't start nothing; won't be nothing."

They both laugh.

"Wanna get some coffee?" Mr. Collins says.

"Sounds good to me," Arwis says.

They walk to a concession stand, order coffee, and take seats.

"You live here?" Mr. Collins asks.

"No, now I live in New York. In Queens. You too, right?" Arwis responds.

"Right! How did you know?" Mr. Collins asks.

"Lucky guess! You're into basketball, right?" Arwis throws another surprise his way.

"Right again. Say you're pretty good. You a psychic or something?" Mr. Collins asks jokingly.

Arwis replies, "No, I'm a movementor."

Looking puzzled, Mr. Collins asks, "A movementor?"

Arwis says, "I'm involved with the Family Restoration Movement."

"What is that about?" Mr. Collins asks.

Arwis replies, "It's a movement to restore black families."

Mr. Collins pauses and looks off as if in deep thought.

Arwis says, "You're separated, right?"

Mr. Collins, looking perplexed, says, "How do you know so much about me?"

Arwis says, "I told you, I'm a Family Restoration Movementor."

"Yes, but that doesn't explain how you know so much about me, " Mr. Collins says.

"I do surveys for my company of children in various schools. You see, Mr. Collins, seventy percent of black children in inner-city schools are from one-parent families," Arwis says.

Mr. Collins says, "Really? My son told you about me?"

"I did a survey at your son's school of what inner city school children wish for most. Your son was in the group that I surveyed. The number one wish was, 'For my family to be back together,'" Arwis says.

"Did you say seventy percent?" Mr. Collins asks.

Arwis nods. "Seventy percent."

"I knew that there was a percentage of children of one-parent families, but I had no idea that the number was that high," Mr. Collins says, frowning.

Arwis says, "Here's something else that you might not know. Seventy percent of inmates in prison are from one-parent families, and seventy percent of those are black men and women, boys and girls. That's why I'm involved with the Family Restoration Movement. We're trying to do something about that. Listen, I have to make a quick call to let some people know that I will be delayed. I'll see you on the plane."

Arwis gets up and leaves Mr. Collins sipping his coffee.

***

Dawson is still in the hearing room, immersed in the conversation going on between him and Mr. Collins.

"Mr. Collins, you said that Arwis told you that he conducted a survey at your son's school," Dawson says.

"That's right," Mr. Collins says.

Dawson says, "Your son attends Emmanuel Junior School in Queens. Isn't that correct?"

"Yes, sir," Mr. Collins says.

Dawson says, "When was this survey done?"

Mr. Collins says, "He didn't say when, but he did say that he conducted the surveys for the National Consortium of Family Associations, of which his company, FPI, is a member."

Ms. Clark says, "Commissioner Dawson, I remember those surveys, sir. I didn't attend it when it was done in my school, but I remember them being done over a six-week period at several schools around the city. It was about eleven months ago. Sir, this could be the answer to the question of how Arwis was able to determine which men to contact about Family Restoration."

Dawson says, "Ms. Clark, please follow up on that to find out who conducted those surveys."

Ms. Clark, "Yes, sir."

Dawson says, "Please continue, Mr. Collins."

"Well, strangely enough, when we boarded the plane, it turned out that we were seated next to each other. At this point, I felt comfortable talking to him. I was now really curious

about the family restoration idea, so after take-off, I asked Arwis to tell him more about the movement. 'The movement is really about you,' he said. 'So, the best way for you to understand it is to understand how you feel about your situation.' Then he said, 'Think about it for a minute, and then tell me what you think was the cause of your marriage failing.' So I did. I thought about it for a few minutes, and then I said…"
***

Flight 717 finally takes off with Mr. Collins in the company of Arwis.

Mr. Collins says, "Now that I think about it, one of the things that I think caused my marriage to fail was the fact that 'I was not raised with the knowledge of what it was to be a good husband or to be a good father.'"

Arwis says, "No one was raised with that knowledge. Most of that has to be lived and experienced."

Mr. Collins says, "I didn't really know what making a marriage work was about. Do you know what I'm saying? I mean, when I was growing up, I had no positive role models in my life. And most of my friends came up the same way. Maybe one or two of them at the most had their mother and father living with them; the rest of us had only mom. Some had a mom and a stepfather, or mom and a boyfriend, or mom and a bunch of different men friends, but very few lived with both their real parents."

Arwis says, "If you have no idea of how to be a man, or a father or a husband, and then you go and jump into marriage, it's a good bet that it won't work out.

Mr. Collins says, "She didn't know anything about being a wife or a mother either. We both came from single-parent families, and we both had a "me" mentality. For us, it was about me, my, mine. Then we had a child early, so there was no time for us to grow amongst each other, to get a real understanding of each other. I still wanted to run with the fellows and be in the clubs hanging out. My idea of being a man was about having a wife at home and a bunch of women on the outside. The women all knew that I was married, but they didn't care. I was not feeling my worth at home due to my youth and inexperience and the pressures and stresses of marriage, which I was ill-equipped to handle. Those women gave me a false sense of worth. And I fed into it. I wouldn't have married any of them. They were dealing with a married man; I knew I could never trust them. The woman who was worthy is the woman that I married. The woman whom I scarred and emotionally abused to the point where it became unbearable and probably irreparable.

Arwis asks, "Did you fight with her?"

Mr. Collins says, "No, I was not a woman beater, but I abused her verbally and emotionally. It wasn't all bad; there were some good times in the beginning. I loved her; I knew that. It might not seem like it, but I did love her. I still love her. I think I will always love her. She abused me, too. This was not a fault of hers but rather evidence of her lack of knowledge of how to treat a man. We never recognized each other for who we were...."

"Did your father die early in your life?" Arwis asks.

Mr. Collins says, "No. He was just never around."

"Were your parents ever married?" Arwis asks.

Mr. Collins says, "No. My father came into my life when I was about sixteen, and then he came as a friend, not as a father."

"Did he marry again?" Arwis asks.

Mr. Collins replies, "No. As I look back, I see that he had a lot of issues in his life, too. I have a sister that I never got to know who did not acknowledge him because he neglected her. He neglected all of his children. When he came around, he came wanting to be my partner. I had friends; I wanted a father."

Arwis then asks, "Who raised you?"

"My mother and my sister. They made sure that I had all the best clothes and all that, and they would constantly instill, 'Oh, he's so cute, he's so fine, he's going to have all the women.' This was preconditioning. You know, I thought the more women I had, the more it validated my manhood, which, now I know, was wrong. It was totally wrong," Mr. Collins says.

"So, the word 'sacred' did not apply in your relationship, huh?" Arwis retorts.

"No. We didn't know that marriage was to be considered sacred. We were so young and immature that we didn't even know what sacred meant. That combination was not good for our young marriage to survive. We both recognize it now, though," Mr. Collins responds.

"How old were you when you got married?" Arwis asks.

"I was married at twenty years old, fresh out of the service," Mr. Collins says.

Arwis throws another question at him, asking, "How old were you when you had your first child?"

"I was twenty-six or seven when I had my first son. But I still didn't recognize my issues at that time. My issues were not recognized until my family was gone. I recognized them when I had to live with my own demons," Mr. Collins answers.

Arwis further probes, asking, "So, you're not pointing your finger at anybody: the circumstances, the environment?"

"Oh no, I can't blame anybody. I can't blame her. If I'm going to blame anybody, I gotta blame myself," Mr. Collins says.

"You know, Mr. Collins, this is a new perspective on the issue of why our black relationships have failed. Most guys put the blame on their women," Arwis says.

Mr. Collins says, "Women have issues that need to be recognized, too. Women who grow up in single-parent households with independent mothers are very strong and adamant themselves. They've seen their mothers raise them and their siblings with no man around. They have the 'I can do it by myself as my mother did it by herself' mindset and conditioning."

Arwis says, "It's really not fair for women to have to raise children alone. Although many of them today think that they can do it alone, they don't realize how wrong it is."

"I'm fearful for my son. My mother had my fear of her in her favor while raising me. I still fear my mother. I mean, I wasn't afraid of her. It was that I felt a sense of reverence towards her. My son doesn't have that for his mother. Most young people today don't. My son has access to things that I didn't have access to at his age. With each generation, it gets worse and worse and more dangerous. I fear the system for my son's sake. I wasn't involved in a system that told me that if my mother spanked my ass, I could call an agency to come and get her. I wasn't affected by all this psychological poisoning that society is giving our kids today. And you know what, the way society is going, the destructiveness is going to get more intense, and it's going to affect kids at younger and younger ages. I really wish I was more involved in raising my children. Unfortunately, it didn't happen that way," Mr. Collins says and pauses for a moment, pondering.

He then picks up again, saying, "Now I see that the deterioration of my relationship was ninety-five percent my fault. I couldn't communicate with her then the way I can now because, at that time, I just didn't know how to. If we got into an argument, my thing would be F--- you or to hell with you. That's how I handled things."

Arwis says, "Even if you knew that you were wrong about something or that she was right?"

"I wouldn't be fair. I wouldn't cop to anything. My macho just would not allow me to admit to anything, and that stupid macho wrong and strong attitude was one of the major causes for the destruction of my marriage. I regret having lost my family, though, not only for the happiness lost but for how I short-changed my kids," Mr. Collins says.

"Do you think that you and your wife were short-changed also?" Arwis questions.

Mr. Collins replies, "No question about it; we all lost out. I think my daughter is going to follow in her mother's footsteps, and my son is going to follow in mine, and that's not good." Mr. Collins frowns.

"You think so?" Arwis asks to make sure Collins means what he is saying.

Mr. Collins says, "I know so. I know from listening to my daughter and communicating with her, and from the nature of our disagreements and disputes, and from listening to my son and knowing his mindset."

Arwis questions, "How old is your son now?"

Mr. Collins replies, "He's sixteen years old now. I'm trying to instill the right things in his head right now."

"Does he hear it?" Arwis asks.

"He hears what I'm saying, but will he heed it? I never heard it. There was no male figure in my life to tell me what I should or shouldn't do. I never heard it. I just did what I wanted to do. My mother did her best with me. She tried. I just couldn't hear her. No discredit to my mother whatsoever," Mr. Collis says seriously.

Arwis adds his two cents, saying, "You know, for women to have to raise boys, or girls too for that matter, by themselves is so unfair to the women and to the children, because the father type questions that sorely need to be answered cannot be answered by the mother."

"Right! I never had a conversation with my mother about sex. I learned about sex on the streets. I never had anybody to sit me down and tell me about the birds and the bees. I only have one father/son memory. He came to one basketball game when I was in elementary school," Mr. Collis adds.

Arwis takes over, asking, "You have a vivid memory of that?"

"Yes, I guess I remember it because it was my only memory of a fun time with him. He didn't care about me, and he didn't want me. I don't think he ever really wanted me. My mother had to take him to court to force him to pay child support for me," Mr. Collis answers, then becomes silent. He drops his head, looking forlorn.

Arwis, with a keen look, asks, "Are you alright?"

"Yeah, I'm alright," says Mr. Collins. "I was just thinking that for a child to grow into manhood on his own without a father is not a good thing. Now I'm a grown man, a husband in name only, a father as best as I can be now, considering and still a hurting child inside. I try not to think about it. I always do, though, and it is really painful, the absence of my kids, of my family. It hurts." He pauses.

Arwis says, "Why don't you join the movement?"

Mr. Collins, surprised, says, "What?"

"Join the movement, restore your family. Don't you want to? Don't you desire to be in your son's life in a significant way now?" Arwis asks.

"Yes, I even desire to be in my wife's life, but it's a fantasy. It's too late now," Mr. Collis says.

Arwis replies, "Not really."

"We've scarred each other too much. The trust factor is so low. We've been separated about nine years…" Mr. Collis frowns.

Arwis retorts, "Families that have been separated for longer than that have been restored."

Mr. Collins looks off into space ponderous again.

Arwis chimes again. "Join the movement. There is hope for your family. It seems that one of the most painful things in your life was the thought that your father didn't want you. Well, do you know that your son may be thinking the same thing about you now?"

Mr. Collins doesn't answer.

"You don't have to make the same mistake that your father made. When it comes to families and children, it is better to want and not have than to have and not want. You have to want to. You will have the support of the Creator, the movement, all of the Movementors, FPI, and the Collective Love," says Arwis.

Mr. Collins finally says, "I've gotta hit the head; be right back."

Mr. Collins gets up and starts to make his way to the back of the plane.

Chapter 4-Page 30 Movementor Information

Taking a glance over everyone present in the hearing room, Mr. Collins says, "Believe it or not, when I came back to my seat, Arwis was not there. This family symbol pin was in my seat. It was attached to a note that had only two words on it. The note said, 'WANT TO.' For the life of me, I could not figure out how he got off that plane. I was the first one off, and I waited by the door for all of the passengers to deplane. Arwis never came off the plane."

Dawson replies, "How long after that did you wait before you made contact with your wife and family?"

Mr. Collins says, "It took me about a week to get my head clear and drum up enough courage to speak to my wife about it. When I finally called her, she said that she was hoping to hear from me. I was so happy I cried. We both did. We had a long talk. We actually dated for about a month, and then we found ourselves back in love. It's been uphill ever since. We're very happy now. I think my son is the happiest. Then I joined the movement and started working for FPI."

Dawson asks, "What do you do at FPI?"

Mr. Collins says, "I'm one of a team of planners for family events. We plan sports events like basketball and golf tournaments, educational training sessions, and entertainment events like talent showcases, concerts, dances, meetings, and dinners."

"These educational training sessions, are the children of the Movementors involved in these sessions? Asks Dawson.

Mr. Collins answers, "Yes, they are. All of the Movementors and their children participate in the sessions. As you know, the methods used are quite effective in developing academic proficiency."

Dawson further probes, saying, "Could you be more specific about these methods? Could you tell us what some of them are and how they work?"

Mr. Collins, in response, says, "I've told you as much as I can about that. What I can tell you is that these methods are used by the Movementors to strengthen their Families and make them more socially, economically, and educationally viable."

Dawson adds, "Mr. Collins, surely you agree that the development of any methods or procedures that can produce the kind of results that we have witnessed in your children should be made available for the benefit of all children."

"Because the inner city schools are continually failing to provide minority children with adequate education, the methods that we use as educational supplements were developed. These methods make it possible for Movementors to provide what their children are not getting in the schools," Mr. Collins says.

Dawson replies, "I personally feel that what you have done is very commendable. However, there are those who feel that it is un-American for your organization to refuse to share the information concerning whatever methods are being used. They feel that all parents and children should have access to that information."

Mr. Collins says, "Sir if you ask yourself the question, 'Why are the inner city schools, which are predominantly attended by people of color, failing?' and give yourself an honest answer, you would undoubtedly glean the information as to why we are doing what we are doing. The schools are not failing because our children are not learning. Our children are not learning because the schools are failing."

Dawson says, "I would assess there to be a number of reasons why inner city schools are failing."

Mr. Collins replies, "I agree, there are a number of reasons why the schools are failing, but would you agree with my assessment of what those reasons are?"

Dawson says, "I don't know exactly what your assessment of those reasons is. And to be honest, if I did know, it's possible that I may or may not agree."

"Just as I thought, Mr. Dawson, but whether you would or would not agree with my assessment really doesn't matter. What does matter is that because the schools are failing, we must do what we are doing. And further, what you and others feel about our controlling who gets to know exactly what we're doing and how we're doing it doesn't matter either. What does matter is that we know that you know and must agree that what we are doing is not failing," Mr. Collins replies.

Dawson says, "That is precisely our point, because the methods that you are using are not failing, is all the more reason why others who are experiencing failure should have access to your more successful methods."

"If you feel that way, why don't you insist that the Hooked On Phonics program, which is heralded to be the absolute best program for teaching reading skills, be used in the public school curriculum in grades one through six? Isn't it "un-American" for the organization that developed that method to sell it to the public instead of sharing it? You know, 'What's good for the goose,' and all that…" Mr. Collins says.

Dawson answers, "That product was developed by a private company to be sold on the commercial market. The free enterprise system and American patent and copyright laws provide private companies the right to do that. On the other hand, and please correct me if I'm wrong, the Family Restoration Movement is not a private commercial company, is it?"

"You're quite right, sir. The Family Restoration Movement is not a private commercial company, but FPI, Family Promoters Incorporated, developed the methods that are being used by the Movementors. Therefore, that same free enterprise system and those same American Patent and Copyright laws provide FPI with those same rights, and because the Family Restoration Movementors work for FPI, they are entitled to company information that non-employees are not entitled to. Will you respect that?" Mr. Collins asks.

Dawson says, "I will, but I must say that seems like a sneaky way to exclude everyone else. Could your reluctance to share be racially motivated? Is this a racial thing? Are only black people privy to this information?"

"We are not reluctant to share, and it is a racial thing in that we are primarily concerned with black people, and yes, at the present time, only black people have access to this information. However, that's only because, at the present time, there are only black people involved in the movement. There are also black people that are not privy to this information simply because they are not yet involved with the movement," Mr. Collins adds.

Dawson says, "Forgive me for saying so, but it sounds like you might be slightly paranoid. Don't you trust your own people?"

Mr. Collins replies, "I can assure you, sir, that we certainly do not consider ourselves to be paranoid. In a movie called, 'Three Days of the Condor,' there was a CIA within the CIA, a sub-group operating inside this organization with its own agenda. This kind of thing happens in real life, too. Remember Watergate? Remember the covert operations of Ollie North? We have to be careful, even of our own people."

"Hmmm." Dawson ponders.

Collins explains, "Malcolm X's movement to improve the quality of life of black people, "by any means necessary," fell apart after his death at the hands of black people. It's been said that Martin Luther King Jr. may have been killed by a black man. Martin's "non-violent movement" also fell apart after his death. It's thought by many that John and Robert Kennedy were killed because they were too interested in improving the quality of life for people of color. Many movements have been stopped cold through the use of this "Kill the head of a snake and the body dies' ' strategy. The Family Restoration Movement is not dependent on one person. Since there is no one leader, this movement cannot be stopped by the death of any one man. All of the Movementors are the leaders. Their commitment to being supportive of all other Movementors and their families adds to the "collective love" and increases the probability for all of us to be successful. Therefore, we must know that those that we share certain information with are truly committed to our cause. We're not being paranoid, just careful.``

Dawson is slightly flustered, and looks of astonishment are evident on the faces of the panel.

Dawson begins to speak, "Mr. Collins, I'm sure that you understand that as Commissioner of the Board of Education, I have a vested interest in having full knowledge of all things that impact the children that attend Bd. of Ed. Schools."

Mr. Collins says, "I do understand your interest, sir. However, I must again say that I have told you all that I can."

Dawson replies, "Thank you, Mister Collins; you may step down."

Dawson covers his microphone again and confers briefly with the panel. He clears his throat and says, "That will conclude the hearings for today. We will continue with the hearings tomorrow morning at 10 a.m. sharp."

The men begin to leave the room and discover that somehow the press has gotten wind of the hearings, and there is a large group of reporters waiting in the hall outside the hearing room. The reporters attempt to get statements from them as to what is going on. The men, however, refuse to make any comments. This does not sit well with the reporters, and they begin to make negative statements.

Reporter number 1 says, "Excuse me, sir; my name is Perkins with The Times. We were told that this is another race-related movement aimed at the white establishment and alleging that minority children are not receiving a quality education. Is this another one of those hate whitey movements?"

Jimmy Parker, a fifty-eight-year-old writer, stops and addresses the reporter's question. He says, "We're not interested in making a lot of statements to the press; however, I will tell you that you have been misinformed. We are concerned about our futures. The future of our families over the next five hundred or so years. Our movement is not focused on hate, revenge, or anything negative.

What we have to do is persevere while we strive to make life what we think it should be for our families," he says with determination.

Chapter 5 - Follow the Leader

Once Jimmy stopped talking, another reporter asks, "We were told that your leader refuses to be interviewed. Could you tell us why that is? Does he have something to hide?"

Mr. Collins starts to respond to the reporter's question but is stopped by Jimmy. Other reporters are throwing questions at the men in a frenzy. No one responds, and they continue to make their way out of the building.

***

Outside the court building, Mr. Collins, Jimmy, and two other men are in the parking lot approaching their car. They are talking among themselves. As they get into the car, a conversation sparks.

Mr. Collins says, "Can you believe this? Here we are doing something that is good, and they think we are up to something negative."

Jimmy says, "You know that there are those in low and high places in this society that don't want us to have the kind of success that we're having."

Charles chimes in, saying, "You would think that they would want minorities to become less dependent on the system for survival, to be more productive and self-sufficient."

Jimmy says, "That's true for other groups but not for us."

Mr. Collins adds, "It's like I said inside, when Martin Luther King's movement grew to such a large scale, he was assassinated. When Malcolm X was assassinated, his movement lost its momentum also. Arwis doesn't want our movement to be stopped like that."

Jimmy replies, "Yeah, you're right. It's that kill the head and the body dies strategy. That's why Arwis always says that we are all leaders of the movement."

Charles says, "I don't blame him for not talking to them. What we can tell them is all they need to know."

Peter Johnston, aka Pete, the fourth man in the car, is a twenty-two-year-old rapper who has not yet given any testimony and says, "Now I don't want to tell them shit. I think they up to something."

Jimmy says, "Hold on, young blood. I think Charles is right; you should testify anyway. I think our testifying is the best way to make it clear that our intentions are positive. We will just tell them what we want them to know, only positive stuff."

Mr. Collins says, "I think he's right. The more we make them see that the movement has no one leader, the more they will stop focusing on Arwis."

Jimmy says, "Let's go to FPI. If Arwis is there, we can tell him what's going on now and see what he says."

The car pulls to a stop in front of the Family Promoters Inc. building. Three of the men get out. Jimmy, driving, says, "If Arwis is here, brief him as to what's going on. I'll be back in about half an hour."

The three men head into the building. Jimmy pulls off, and a car parked on the other side of the street pulls off behind him. In the car, there are two men dressed in black suits who strike the image of government agents. One speaks into a handheld radio.

The agent says, "Three of them went into the building. We are following the fourth. We will bring him in for questioning."

Jimmy stops at a light. The agent's car pulls up alongside. One of the agents comes over to Jimmy's car and shows him his ID.

The agent says, "Excuse me, sir; my name is Agent Galloway with the Secret ServiceSecret Service. We would like you to come with us to headquarters to answer some questions."

Jimmy snaps. "Questions about what?"

The agent says, "Please, sir, it will only take a short time. We would appreciate your cooperation."

"Okay," Jimmy says.

The agent goes around and gets into the car with Jimmy. He waves his partner on, turns to Jimmy, and says, "Please follow my partner."

Jimmy almost yells, "What is this all about?"

"Please be patient, sir; my boss will answer all of your questions," the agent says,

They arrive at the government building and proceed into an underground garage, where they part and exit their cars, leading Jimmy to the elevator.

Jimmy says, "Are you going to tell me what this is all about? What does the   Secret Service want with me?"

The agent replies, "Patience, Mr. Parker. Everything will be explained to you in just a few minutes."

As they enter the elevator, Jimmy asks, "How do you know my name?"

The agents don't answer. The elevator doors open on the third floor, and one of the agents says, "Right this way, Mr. Parker."

They lead Jimmy into an office and offer him a seat.

The agent says, "Please have a seat. Someone will be right with you."

Jimmy shrugs, sits down, and begins to look around. After a few minutes, the Secret Service director, Robert Grant, enters the room. He is relatively young-looking, considering the scope of his position. He is dressed in a white shirt and tie and black slacks. He introduces himself to Jimmy, saying, "Thank you for coming in, Mr. Parker. My name is Robert Grant. I am the director of the Secret Service. We really appreciate your cooperation."

Jimmy says, "Just what is it that the Secret ServiceSecret Service wants of me?

Director Grant says, "There is no cause for alarm, Mr. Parker. We are actually interested in talking to the person who calls himself Arwis. We have made several attempts to contact him, but as of yet, we have not been able to do so. We have been given information that he is the leader of some kind of movement. When we hear "movement," flags go up, and we have to check things out."

Jimmy says, "I understand that the word "movement" has strong connotations, but I can assure you that we are involved in a peaceful movement."

Director Grant, "You will forgive me, Mr. Parker, but I have never heard of a peaceful movement."

Jimmy, smiling slightly, says, "Do you have a dictionary, sir?"

Director Grant presses a button on his desk intercom and says, "Desiree, would you please bring me a dictionary?"

The voice on the other end says, "Right away, Mr. Grant."

The director's secretary, a lovely young woman of about twenty-eight, enters the room but does not see Jimmy standing by the window. She hands the director the dictionary and affectionately caresses his hand. The director moves his hand and looks at Jimmy, who has seen this display of tenderness. The secretary is startled at the sight of Jimmy, excuses herself, and leaves. Jimmy walks over and sits down again. The director appears embarrassed and begins to flip through the pages as Jimmy speaks.

Jimmy says, "We apply the fourth meaning of the word to our movement."

Director Grant, reading, says, "Hmmm. A complete or radical change of any kind {a *movement* in modern physics."

Jimmy continues to say, "Our movement is focused on radically changing things that impact our families. We are mainly focusing on restoring our broken families, improving our economy, and improving the quality of our children's education. As I said, our movement is of a peaceful nature. It is truly a shame that in the year 2003, there were children in the seventh grade with first-grade reading levels. How in the hell can a child in America in 2003 be in the 7th grade and have a first-grade reading level?"

Director Grant says, "I would say that much of the fault for that would rest with that child's parents."

Jimmy says, "Well, a lot of things come into play - things that on the surface don't give you a clue as to how they factor into the equation, but the absence of them has a major impact on our lives and the lives of our children, especially, on the lives of our children. And the sad truth is that too many of today's youth don't have the benefit of these things working for them."

Director Grant says, "What things are you talking about?"

"Remember the truant officer and the left-back policy? Remember yes, mam, and no, sir? Remember, thank you, excuse me, and please, and so many other seemingly unimportant things; things that really help to shape our character and bear significantly on our skills and abilities and our development. Remember honesty and truth. Remember *knowledge* of and love for God. You know, "Family" type things," Jimmy says.

Director Grant says, "That's my point; these things are primarily the responsibility of the parents, the family."

Jimmy replies, "But that's my point. There are so many young people that have no 'family.' So many are being cheated because life is about 'family,' and too many don't have the luxury or the benefit of the 'family,' and consequently, they miss out on many of these important developmental things."

Director Grant says, "There are many people who have fared well that were raised by one parent, those who didn't have the benefit of a traditional family that you speak of."

Jimmy retorts, "This is true, but many more have done and will do much better with one. It's very simple. 'Family' is natural. 'Family' is like proton, electron, neutron. It's basic to us all. Unfortunately, many of our people missed certain basics and don't really see the importance of 'family.' There are also forces and powers that aid in the perpetuation of that ignorance.

Director Grant says, "You sound like you are alleging that there is a conspiracy."

Jimmy says, "A conspiracy is a secret plan. It is no secret that since the days of Willie Lynch, some 450 years ago, a concerted effort has been and is still being made to keep dissension, confusion, and separation of our families in place."

Director Grant asks, "Just who are you accusing today for what happened 450 years ago?"

Jimmy says, "Today, I am not accusing anybody of anything. What I am doing is making every effort to improve the quality of life of our families. Why are you opposing this when you well know that minority people are systematically denied the rights and privileges that would allow them to gain a fair number of top-level positions in government, education, employment, politics, housing, you name it?"

Director Grant says, "Again, I say, who are you blaming for this?"

Jimmy replies, "Although we have been wronged by others across the board, one of my pet peeves is with my own people. As Brother Malcolm X put it, 'Too many of us have been tricked, hoodwinked, bamboozled, run amuck, led astray, and brainwashed so badly that we don't even realize how big a role we are playing in hurting ourselves.'"

Director Grant says, "Are you trying to blame someone else for what you are doing to yourselves? Are you trying to blame someone else for your people degrading themselves?"

Jimmy says, "With all due respect, we are not fixed on placing blame for anything on anyone anymore. Fate pays credit where credit is due. What we know is that our past experiences and present needs have us focused on what we can do now to strengthen our family relationships and make our futures better than our past. Is there any problem with that?"

Director Grant replies, "Based on what you have told me, I don't see a problem. However, I would still very much like to speak with your leader, Arwis."

"As was told to Commissioner Dawson, Arwis is not the leader of the Family Restoration Movement. According to him, he merely started it for us. We, the movementors, are all leaders. You see, the motto of the movement is "Father And Mother, I Love You," and since we are all Fathers, that makes us all leaders of the movement to restore our Families. Get it? We're all leaders," Jimmy retorts.

Director Grant, looking a bit perplexed, says, "Nevertheless, we would like to speak with him anyway. Could you arrange for us to meet with him?"

Jimmy replies, "I'm sorry, sir, but I cannot promise you that I can do that. If you have no other questions for me, I would like to leave. I have a business to attend to."

Director Grant, now annoyed, says, "I must inform you that the hearings will no longer be conducted by the Board of Education but by my agency. We will subpoena Arwis to testify if we have to."

Jimmy says, "I'm sure that that is your prerogative, sir. I am also sorry, but again, I must say that I am not able to promise you a meeting with him. Now, again, if there is nothing more, I would like to leave."

Director Grant says, "Before you leave, could you explain the meaning or significance of that pin that you all wear?"

Jimmy, smiling broadly, replies, "I will be glad to. It is the (FPI) logo and also the Family Restoration Movement symbol. When Arwis explained its significance to us, it gave us all a clearer understanding of the importance of restoring and maintaining our families. May I have a pencil and a pad? I can demonstrate its significance much better graphically."

"Certainly," replies Director Grant. He hands Jimmy the materials, and Jimmy begins to illustrate and explain the logo.

Director Grant says, "That is remarkable. Really remarkable! Thank you for coming in and being so cooperative. You may leave. My office will be in touch with you."

Jimmy leaves the office by the rear door that he came in through.

Director Grant presses his intercom, then says, "Deseree, would you please come in here?"

The voice on the other end of the telecom says, "Yes, sir."

Deseree enters the office, apologizing. She says, "I'm sorry, Bob, I didn't know that anyone was here."

Their eyes meet as she walks toward him, and he looks at her up and down. They are about to embrace.***

Chapter 6 - A brother helps a son rise

One week later, the hearing room in the Secret Service building is arranged similarly to the hearing room in one scene from the movie "The Godfather." Director Grant and a panel of four others are behind a long table with another table facing it for the people giving testimony; behind this table is an audience of reporters, Movementors, and spectators.

"Will Mr. Peter Johnston please come forward?" the clerk calls out.

Peter Johnston, the twenty-two-year-old rapper, is flashily dressed and has the family symbol pin on the front of his cap that he has on backward.

The clerk asks, "Would you please remove your hat and state your name?"

Re-Pete says, "My name is Peter Johnston, aka Re-Pete."

Director Grant says, "Re-Pete?"

Re-Pete responds, "Right! When I started in the rap game, I was known as McPete, but after my third song was a hit, I changed my name to Re-Pete. You know, hit after hit. *NORDUM SANE.*"

Director Grant says, "Yes, I understand. I seem to remember reading about you having had some serious trouble about a year ago. It had to do with a shooting and a lawsuit against you and your record company, Bad Butt Productions.:

Re-Pete says, "I'm not down with Bad Butt Productions no more. After that drama, I broke and got down with Family Promoters Inc., and now I spit on my own label called "Wised Up.""

Director Grant says, "Would you tell us how you met Arwis, the leader of the movement? And how did you get involved with this family restoration movement, and how you came to be with Family Promoters Inc.?"

Re-Pete says, "No problem. At first, when that static jumped off, I didn't think it was my fault at all, but then I kicked it with Arwis, and I began to see things a little differently, you know. I'm sorry for what happened. I'm sorry that people died unnecessarily. I lost my brother too, you know."

Director Grant replies, "Yes, I know. Unfortunately, there have been many incidents of violence in which lives were lost and people suffered that are directly connected to this rap music. Yet many of the people in that industry insist that they are getting a bad rap, no pun intended. "

Re-Pete responds, saying, "No, Big Pun didn't die because of any violence."

Director Grant says, "When I say pun, I mean..."

Light laughter is heard in the room, and the director bangs his gavel. Re-Pete looks around, wondering what's funny.

Director Grant says, "Well, never mind. Many people feel that the content...the subject matter of the rap music is negatively influential, that it causes the young people who listen to it to do bad things."

Re-Pete says, "Oh, yeah. I'm hip to that now. Like I said, after I kicked it with Arwis, I started seeing things differently. Let me break it down for you. About a year and a half ago, I did a concert in LA. After the concert, me and my man, Cool Tee, were going to hang out. Tee came to my dressing room and told me that he had a couple of hot honeys that wanted to hang with us. So I said, 'Bet, let's do it. Let's get it poppin.' I didn't know that they had come to the concert with some dudes."

Director Grant questions, "Don't you have a wife and family?"

Re-Pete says, "Now I have a wife, but at that time, Shamella was just my shorty. She was the mother of my son. It wasn't all about her then. Yo, cats in the rap game deal with honeys all over. Anyway, after Arwis pulled my coat, I married her. Now it's all about her."

Director Grant says, "Arwis pulled your coat? Re-Pete replies. "Arwis is a deep brother. He set me straight on a bunch of stuff, Nordum Sane?

***

It's nighttime, and Re-Pete has just finished changing his clothes at the Magic Mountain dressing room in LA. Outside the dressing room, Cool Tee is talking to two very pretty and shapely young girls. They look to be about 18 or 19

77

years old. There are many people moving about. Stagehands are loading instrument cases while the security guards are ushering the groupies out and preparing to close the stadium. It is a typical after-concert backstage scene. Outside in the parking lot, two boys are in their vehicle, waiting for the two girls to come out.

***

Standing outside the dressing room door, Cool Tee says, "Yo, y'all wait right here for a minute."

Cool Tee entered the dressing room and said to Re-Pete, "Yo, Ree, I hooked us up with two Thoneys that want to party with us."

Re-Pete says, "They're not like those last two bitches you came with, are they? They were whacked."

Cool Tee says, "No bullshit; these chicks are off the hook. That's my word."

Re-Pete replies, "Well, let's do it. Let's get it poppin. Where's Rakim?"

Cool Tee says, "He's waiting for us in the ride."

Re-Pete, putting on his hat, says, "Let's do this."

They leave the dressing room, and Cool Tee introduces Re-Pete to the two girls, who are tickled pink to be in his company.

Cool Tee says, "Yo, Lisa, Melanie, meet Re-Pete."

Re-Pete, shaking his head in the affirmative, says, "What up?"

They leave the stadium by the rear stage door where Rakim, Re-Pete's bodyguard/driver, is waiting. As they enter Re-Pete's black SUV, they are seen from about fifty yards away by the two boys, Darnell, who is Lisa's brother, and Jermaine, who is her boyfriend. Rakim proceeds to leave the parking lot, and the boys follow them. The boys are visibly angry; both are high on cocaine. Jermaine is on the driver's side of the gray sedan.

Darnell says, "You see that shit, Maine? I thought you said they were going to ask for an autograph."

Jermaine says, "That's what they said, D."

Darnell takes a pistol out of the glove compartment and climbs into the back seat.

Darnell says, "This is fucked up. I don't like being dissed like this. Just follow them. I'll fix this shit."
***

Cocaine and alcohol are being passed around in Re-Pete's car. All are laughing and making small talk. Cool Tee is in the passenger seat, while Re-Pete is in the back seat between the two girls.

Re-Pete says, "Where's the party?"

Rakim replies, "It's over on La Cienega Blvd."

"Are the guys from the LA crew gonna be there?" Re-Pete says.

"Ice Man and Jammer said that they will be there. They want to talk to you about lacing their next joint," Rakim says.

Re-Pete replies, "Ice Man better have my bucks from that last jam."

The cars come to a long stretch of dark highway.

***

Darnell, sitting in the gray sedan, says, "Pull up beside them, Maine."

Jermaine says, "Bet!"

As the sedan comes alongside Re-Pete's SUV, the girls see them and panic. The sedan almost hits them, and Rakim shouts.

Rakim says, "What the fuck is wrong with that asshole?"

Lisa says, "Oh shit, that's Darnell and Jermaine."

"You know them?" Cool Tee asks.

Lisa says, "One of them is my brother."

Re-Pete says, "What the fuck is his problem?"

Darnell rolls down his window and points his pistol at the SUV. Cool Tee sees it and says, "Oh shit, he's got a piece."

Cool Tee takes out his gun as Darnell fires, hitting Cool Tee in the head. He slumps down in his seat. The girls start screaming.

Rakim said, "Get down, Ree!"

The cars jockey for position on the highway. Rakim takes out his gun and returns fire, hitting Jermaine. Darnell fires again, hitting Rakim. Both cars go out of control. The sedan goes off the highway into a ravine and stops. The SUV veers off and hits a light pole. The impact throws Lisa through the front windshield and kills her.

Re-Pete, not being seriously hurt, crawls out of the car and has the presence of mind to throw the vile of cocaine into some nearby brush before the police arrive. He pulls Rakim out of the vehicle and lays him on the grass. Melanie gets out, sits up, and cradles Lisa, crying.

When the police and the ambulance arrive, they find two dead and one injured. Re-Pete, Melanie, and Darnell are shaken but not seriously hurt. Melanie is still crying.
***

Standing in the hearing room of the Secret Service building, answering Director Grant, Re-Pete says, "Me and that girl Melanie and that girl Lisa's brother wasn't hurt that bad, so they took us to the hospital and checked us out; then they took us to the police station and asked us a bunch of questions about what happened."

Director Grant says, "What happened to your bodyguard?"

Re-Pete says, "Oh yeah, Rakim had got shot in his shoulder. They took the bullet out, then the cops questioned him. They didn't do nothing to him, though, cause he had his papers for his piece, and that other kid shot at us first. He went to jail."

Director Grant questions, "Were you charged with anything?"

Re-Pete replies, "Yeah, they gave me a summons for having an open bottle of cognac in my vehicle."

Director Grant asks again, "Were there any drugs found?"

Re-Pete pauses and looks up at the ceiling, remembering what he had done with the vile of cocaine that he had in the car. He snaps out of the daze and says, "The only drugs that was found was on that other kid that Rakim had shot. That was a really bad scene. I never wanted nothing like that to happen, but it wasn't my fault. I didn't know that those girls came with somebody else. I can understand that they was mad, but Yo, they should have never bugged out like that."

Director Grant says, "As I said before, this is the kind of thing that is associated with this whole rap music thing. Studies show that 80% or more of the subject matter of rap material is about guns, drugs, sex, and violence. It is inevitable that young people are going to get into trouble after constantly listening to that kind of stuff."

Re-Pete responds, "I know; that's why I left Bad Butt Productions. I went to that girl Lisa's funeral. My producer told me not to, but I went anyway. I really felt bad about what had happened. I shouldn't have went though cause her parents blamed me for losing their children. One was dead, and the other was in prison. That girl, Lisa, had another brother who said that he was gonna make me pay for the pain that I caused his family. Yo, it was really messed up."

"Do you think that you should have been blamed for what happened?" Director Grant asks.

Re-Pete says, "I didn't think so then."

"You say, then. What do you think now?" Director Grant counters.

Re-Pete replies, "Like I said before. That's why I wound up leaving Bad Butt Productions. That whole thing gave me big problems. I was never involved with anybody getting killed before. I mean, I grew up in the hood, and I've seen a lot of stuff go down, *NORDUM SANE*, but these two people were killed in my ride. I almost lost my life; I lost my brother and almost lost my son. I got a lot of bad publicity. I couldn't write. I lost a lot of gigs. It was hell. I even started to off myself."

Director Grant asks, "Would you tell us about that?"

Re-Pete abruptly says, "Ah-ight. So much bad stuff was going on I started bugging out. That girl Lisa's parents had filed a hundred million dollar lawsuit against me and Bad Butt Productions. They claimed that the stuff that we were recording was causing young people to do a lot of bad things. They claimed that rappers were nothing but a bunch of thugs and criminals and that, like you said, all we rap about is violence, getting fast money, drugs, and sex. They talked about Tupac and Biggie getting killed. About R-kelly having sex with those young girls, about ODB, and a bunch of other rappers all over being arrested for all kinds of stuff. They talked about what happened to Puffy. They talked about a whole lot of stuff.

Anyway, one day, dealing with all this crap had me feeling really bad, and I was thinking that I would just off myself and get away from all the bullshit. That's when Arwis saved me."

"Just how did Arwis save you?" Director Grant asks.

"I had sat up all night at LookOut Point. It's a tourist spot up by Magic Mountain," Re-Pete tells him.

Director Grant says, "Yes, I know. Please continue."

Re-Pete continues to say, "I go there sometimes when I'm feeling rotten. Well, I was standing there looking at a picture of my son and thinking about jumping. Next thing I know, Arwis is standing beside me. I don't know how he got up on me like that without me seeing him, but he was there, and he said…"

***

Outside the Look-Out Point, Re-Pete has been sitting in his car all night, smoking marijuana and thinking. Just before sunrise, he gets out of the car and walks over to the rail overlooking the valley. He is startled by a voice saying, "You can see the son rise much better if you stand closer to the family."

It's none other than Arwis.

Re-Pete, startled, says, "Yo, you scared the shit out of me, man. Who is you? Where did you come from?"

Arwis says, "From where you don't want to go until it's your time."

Re-Pete, backing away, replies, "What? Yo man, I ain't got no time for no bullshit. I think you better step off."

Arwis says, "Andre would have taken care of Jamel if you had gotten killed in that shoot-out, but unfortunately, he was killed, and if you are not around, who is going to raise Jamel? And what about Shamella? You know she loves you. What's going to happen to them?"

Re-Pete says, "Man, who the fuck are you, and how do you know about my family?

Arwis replies, "Some of it I read in the papers. You are Re-Pete the rapper, aren't you?"

Re-Pete says, "Yeah, I'm Re-Pete. Now, who the hell are you?"

"I'm called Arwis," Arwis tells him.

Re-Pete, perplexed, questions, "You said you read some about me in the papers, but you're talking about stuff that wasn't in the papers. Like, how did you know that I was gonna... I mean, how did you know that I was thinking about...and how do you know about my woman and my son?"

Arwis, smiling, says, "I'm involved with a movement called the Family Restoration Movement back in New York, and Shamella came to see me because she is worried about you."

Re-Pete says, "Shamella talked to you about me?"

Arwis replies, "She really loves you, and she knows that you are really hurting about what happened and about your brother. She thought that I might be able to help you."

Re-Pete says, "How can you help me? You don't know what I'm dealing with."

"Oh, but I do. You see, I tried to end it all once too. That's not the way," says Arwis. "It only creates more problems."

Re-Pete, now curious, says, "More problems? More problems for who?"

Arwis says, "That's a long story. I'll tell you about it one day. Now, you need to solve the ones that you are dealing with, and at the same time, you can help a lot of young people avoid a bunch of problems."

Re-Pete snaps. "What the fuck are you talking about?"

Arwis, maintaining his calm, says, "By doing what you do: rapping. Writing and rapping positive stuff for young people to listen to instead of that poison that they are used to. You know what young people deal with, the problems that they have. You could really make a difference. Mace did it. Rev. Run did it. You can do it too. Even on a larger scale than they did. What do you have to lose? You were about to throw it all away anyway."

Re-Pete says, "They could afford to change up and still get paid. Mace was down with Puffy. And Run was down with Russell. Most of the rappers out there would write positive stuff, but the record companies want gangster. If we don't give them what they want, they get rid of us and find someone who will."

Arwis responds, "That sounds like the industry is part of a conspiracy to keep young people's minds messed up and are using you and many others like you to do their dirty work for them. You have to look at the bigger picture."

"We don't want to hurt anybody. We just want to get paid," Re-Pete says.

"Right, and they know it. That's why they offer you a feast of material things that is hard for you to resist. They even tell you that your material is Art and should not be censored. All the while, they know that a lot of the stuff you guys are saying is pure poison to the minds of young people. Especially young people of color," Arwis says.

Re-Pete turns and looks toward the sunrise, visibly contemplating what Arwis has said. He hears Arwis behind him saying, "That's really pretty, but like I said, you can see the son rise much better if you stand closer to the family. Look me up when you get back to New York."

Re-Pete doesn't answer for a moment, and when he turns around, he sees Arwis is not there. He starts to look around and calls out Arwis' name. The sun begins to blare on the windows of his car. Our POV moves closer to the car until we can see Re-Pete waking up in his car, calling to Arwis. It is now that he realizes that he was dreaming. He looks around and finds Arwis' business card on the seat next to him, but no Arwis.

***

Back in the Secret Service hearing room, Re-Pete tells Director Grant, "I know that some of this might sound whacked, but that's how I met Arwis. I came back to New York that day and went to see him at FPI. I don't know how he did it, but he got those people at Bad Butt to give up my contract, and he got that girl Lisa's family to settle their case for 25 million dollars. He helped me to set up a label under Family Productions called Wised Up, and my first record, which is a hit, is called *Stand Closer.* Me and Shamella got married. I'm a family man now, and I'm down with the movement."

Director Grant says, "How did your brother die?"

Re-Pete answers, saying, "I think that girl Lisa's other brother hired some dudes to kill my son. He had said he was gonna make me pay for causing his family pain. A car passed by the park where my son plays, and somebody shot at my son, but my brother was there and jumped in front of my son and got killed. My brother lost his life saving my son."

Director Grant asks, "How do you know that it was Lisa's brother?"

Re-Pete says, "I don't know who it was. The cops never caught anybody, but I think he had something to do with it. I was gonna go after him, but Arwis says to leave it alone and let the cops handle it. He convinced me that the best thing for me to do is to be thankful that I still have my family."

Director Grant says, "That is very sad, but I'd say that that is sound advice."

"I told you that Arwis is a deep brother. He inspired me to write positive stuff like this: DO FOR YOURS
Do for yours and I'll do for mine
This world is like a ladder that we all must climb
We can make moves alone or get down together
To make the future for the youth much better so,

Do for yours and I'll do for mine
And later on down the line
Everything will be fine
So, what are you waiting on,
Get down, get to it
Make moves like Nike and just
DO IT." Re-Pete says as he finishes the rap song.

"Why is it that no one but you movementors ever see Arwis?" Director Grant counters.

Re-Pete retorts, "Why do you want to see him?"

Director Grant says, "Is he afraid to talk to anyone outside of your movement?"

Re-Pete replies, "What do you want to talk to him about? Yo, I guess he don't want to talk to y'all. I don't know."

Director Grant says, "We don't want to have to put out a warrant for him."

Re-Pete says, "Yo, whatever, man! Do what you got to do."

Director Grant says, "Yes, we will. Thank you, Mr. Johnston; that will be all. The hearings will be in recess for one hour."

In the back of the room are seated two well-dressed men named Gennelli and Rizzo, who get up and leave the room. In the hallway outside the hearing room, Gennelli makes a cell phone call.

Gennelli says, "We still don't know how to contact him, sir...Yes, sir, they did ask...

Yes, sir. Mr. Di'Marco, how is your son doing?"

He hangs up the phone.

Rizzo says, "What did he say?"

Gennelli replies, "He said to find Arwis."

Rizzo, seemingly angry, says, "How the hell are we going to find him if the Secret Service can't?"

Gennelli says, "Let's go."

They proceed to exit the building.

Rizzo asks, "How's his kid?"

"Not good. The doctors say that he has to have that transfusion soon, or he's not gonna make it," Gennelli says.

The two men leave the building and head for their car in the parking area outside the Secret Service building. Entering their car, Rizzo says, "Where are we going?"

Gennelli replies, "To the FPI building on Halsey Street."

Rizzo questions, "For what?"

Gennelli takes out his cell phone again and makes another call.

***

Mason's apartment is a standard one that you would typically find in a mid-rise building. Entering it, you step into a modest-sized living room with a couple of windows, allowing a decent amount of natural light to brighten the space. The walls are painted in a neutral color, creating a simple and clean aesthetic. Adjacent to the living room, there is a compact kitchen equipped with essential appliances like a refrigerator, stove, and microwave, along with enough cabinet space for storage. The apartment features two bedrooms, with enough room for a queen or full-sized bed and a small closet in each. There is a shared bathroom, complete with a standard sink, mirror, bathtub, shower, and toilet. The flooring is a combination of laminate and carpet, providing a comfortable underfoot feel. Although his apartment does not have extravagant features, it serves as a functional and comfortable living space.

Mason is talking on the phone to someone to whom he owes money and who is very adamant about hurting him if he does not pay soon. He begs, "I told you I'll have the money soon. You know me; I always pay you."

The voice on the other end says, "You pay, but you're always late. You've got one week, Mason, and one week only."

Before Mason can say something, he hears a BEEP on his phone.

Mason says, "Hold on one second; I have a call coming."

He clicks over then says, "Hello!"

Gennelli is on the phone inside his car. "Mason, yeah, it's me. Listen, meet us at the FPI building in fifteen minutes; the boss has a job for you…Yeah, on Halsey Street," he says.

***

Mason gets back on the call he had put on hold. "Yo, I just got a job. I should have your money tonight. Okay… I'll be there… I said I'll be there!" He snaps.

***

Sitting beside Gennelli in his car is Rizzo. He says, "Why did you call Mason?"

Gennelli says, "Did you hear the director say that no one sees Arwis except the Movementors?"

Rizzo replies, "Yeah, so…?"

Gennelli says, "Yeah, so we're gonna get Mason to join the movement."

Rizzo, taken by surprise, says, "We're gonna what?"

Gennelli replies, "We're gonna get Mason to join the movement. He's black; that way, he'll get to see Arwis. Then he can take him out. You remember that's what happened to Malcolm X. We got black people to deal with that."

Rizzo says, "Why does the boss want him taken out anyway? I don't see why he's so important.

What's he doing wrong?"

Gennelli replies, "He's not doing anything wrong. What he is doing is too much right. Boss said that this movement thing is causing us to lose money big time."

Frowning, Rizzo says, "How's that?"

Gennelli answers, "It's causing black people to get organized. Their children are doing better in school. They're not spending money like they have been. They're still spending, but differently. The drug business has been down since Arwis started this movement thing. The sales of hardcore rap music are going down. Sales of designer clothes are declining. They're involved in what they call selective purchasing, meaning that they are walking that extra block to patronize Black and Latino businesses. Our sources downtown tell us that crime on the streets is going down, and many of them have canceled their life insurance policies with the organization's companies and are buying their policies from FPI Insurance, which Arwis started. And they are saving money. Our sources in the banking industry say that thousands of them have opened new bank accounts in the last six months, and there's probably more stuff happening that hasn't come out yet."

Rizzo says, "Damn! Where did this guy come from?"

Gennelli says, "Did you hear anything about him while you were in jail?"

"No," Rizzo says quickly.

Gennelli replies, "That's the kicker. No one seems to know exactly who he is or where he came from other than the people involved in this movement, and many of them say they met him in a dream. Didn't you hear the story this Re-Pete guy told? There's even talk that this Arwis guy is an Angel. Ha-ha-ha-ha!"

Rizzo is quiet for a moment with a solemn look on his face.

Gennelli asks, "What's the matter?"

Rizzo replies, "What if he is an angel? I mean, for one guy to quietly get so much done before our people knew what was happening, he might be an angel. I don't like the idea of killing no angel."

Gennelli says, "Come on, you don't really believe this guy is an angel, do you? And anyway, we're not gonna do it. We're gonna get Mason to do it. I'll bet he's just another guy. Every so often, some guy decides that he is going to be the savior of his people and tries to change things. You know, like Martin Luther King and Malcolm X. Do you think they were angels?"

Rizzo then replies, "No, but from what you say this guy has done, he is much different from and more dangerous than those two guys put together. He didn't come out marching and protesting; he just started making things happen."

The car pulls up in front of the FPI building, and Gennelli gets out, saying, "There's Mason; wait here."

Rizzo says, "Are you sure you want to do this?"

Gennelli bends over looks in the car window, then says, "Boss said find him and take him out, and that's what we're gonna do. You just wait here and keep the motor running."

Gennelli walks over to Mason, a casually dressed black man about thirty years old, who is standing in front of the FPI building. They talk for a minute; then Gennelli lights a cigarette and watches through the glass doors as Mason enters the FPI building and approaches the reception desk.

The receptionist is a beautiful black girl about twenty-five years old, very smartly dressed and smiling. Her earrings are the FPI symbol.

The receptionist says, "May I help you, sir?"

Mason replies, "I would like to see Mr. Arwis."

"Do you have an appointment?" she asks.

Mason replies, "No."

"What would you like to see him about?" She throws a question again.

Mason responds, "I want to join the movement."

The receptionist tells him, "I'm sorry, sir, but Movementors are recruited."

Just then, one of the elevator doors opens, and three men come out. Two women enter the elevator, and one turns and greets Arwis, who turns around to talk with her.

Mason, who overhears, starts walking toward Arwis, whose back is to him.

The receptionist shouts at him, "EXCUSE ME, SIR! SIR!"

Mason continues walking toward Arwis and pulls out a gun. He raises the gun, and before he fires, he shouts, "GET YOUR HAND OUT OF MY POCKET!"

Before he can fire his weapon, he is jumped from behind by a movementor who has just entered the building. They scuffle, and Mason drops his gun. Gennelli sees this and goes back to his car. Mason breaks away from the revolutionary and runs out of the building.

***

The two men in the car outside the FPI building see Mason as he bumps into a passerby, and two Movementors catch up to him and subdue him. Two young white police officers in a passing patrol car see the scuffle and stop to investigate. The two men in the car drive off.

Gennelli yells, "Damn! That black bastard fucked up."

Rizzo says, "Do you think he did it?"

Gennelli replies, "Did you hear a shot? He fucked up; that's what happened. Boss is not gonna be happy about this."

***

Two police officers bring Mason into the 110 Precinct Station to be booked. A detective sees him and makes a phone call to the same person that Gennelli had called. He is talking in a low voice so as not to be overheard.

The detective says, "Two rookies just brought Mason into the station in handcuffs. What's going on?"

The voice on the other side of the phone says, "He was supposed to handle a job. Gennelli and Rizzo said he blew it. Feinberg is on his way over there."

The detective says, "Right." He then hangs up the phone and walks over to the two rookies.

The detective says, "What do we have here?"

Rookie One says, "This guy attempted to shoot someone at the FPI building. Didn't get a chance to, though; some employees chased him out before he could even get a shot off."

Mason recognizes the detective as one on the take. He stares at him as if to say, "Get me out of here."

The detective speaks, saying, "Give me his papers. I'll take him down to booking."

He takes the papers from the rookie, grabs Mason by the arm, and proceeds to escort him off. He takes Mason into one of the interrogation rooms and begins to question him.

At the interrogation room, Mason stands, agitated. "Take these damn cuffs off me," he yells.

The detective, removing cuffs, says, "What happened?"

Mason replies, "Some guy jumped me as I was about to…" He stops mid-sentence as the door to the room opens, and the rookie officer enters.

The rookie officer says, "This guy would not give his name. I'll have to run his prints to find out who he is."

The detective says, "Leave it to me; I'll handle it."

"Yes, sir," replies the rookie.

As the rookie is leaving, the organization's lawyer, Joel Fienberg, enters the room.

Fienberg says, "I want my client released immediately. It seems that someone forgot to read him his rights."

"You know he'll have to be arraigned first, counselor," replies the detective.

Feinberg says, "Sit tight, Mason, and don't say anything. I'll have you out in an hour."

About an hour later, Mason is released from the 110 Precinct. As he and Fienberg leave the station, we hear Fienberg say, "He's waiting for your call. See you around."

Fienberg then walks away. Mason pulls out his cell phone and makes a call.

The voice on the other end says, "Secret Service, Bronson speaking; how may I help you?"

Mason replies, "This is Mason; let me speak to Mr. Grant."

Bronson says, "Hold on."

Director Grant gets on the call, saying, "Mason, why are you calling me here?"

Mason replies, "We have to talk. We have a problem."

"Meet me at the usual place in an hour," Director Grant orders.

Mason, submissive, says, "Right."

Mason's car enters the Queens Center Mall parking lot, goes up to the second level, and parks next to Director Grant's car. Mason exits his car and gets into the back seat of Grant's car.

Grant says, "What happened?"

"Gennelli called me and said that Mr. D wanted me to hit this guy Arwis at FPI," Mason informs.

"How did you get out of it?" Grant inquires.

Mason says, "I shouted something before I fired to alert him. Someone jumped me, and that saved him."

Grant replies, "That was quick thinking, but you were lucky. You could have been shot."

Mason, frowning, says, "I know. I was wearing a vest. I had to do something; I couldn't just shoot the guy."

"Did you see his face?" Grant asks.

Mason says, "No."

"How do you know that it was him?" Grant asks.

Mason answers, "I heard a woman speak to him."

Grant says, "You know that they are going to try again, and we can't protect him because we don't know who he is. We've got to find that guy."

Mason says, "They don't know who he is either. He's really good. He's avoiding them and us."

Grant adds, "Well, at least you didn't blow your cover. What about the drug deal?"

Mason says, "It's supposed to go down tonight. I'll get back to you."

Grant responds, "If all goes well, we will nail Di'Marco tonight. Don't call me at the office again."

"Be there when the deal goes down, and I won't have to call you," Mason says as he gets out of the car. Grant sees him off, saying, "Good luck."

Chapter 7-Page 52 Arwisville

At the FPI Auditorium at night, a large crowd of Movementors gathered to hear Arwis speak.

Arwis finally speaks up. "The time has come for me to share something with you about myself. I was a troubled and very unhappy youth and caused my family much trouble. Although I was a very bright kid and had a lot of skill and talent, I was not able to put them to the best use. I always felt sad and angry about not having my father around. I had a stepfather who was not a bad guy, but I didn't really appreciate him at the time. I loved and needed my mother, but in the back of my mind, I blamed her for me not having my father. I never really found out exactly why they broke up, but I blamed them both for not keeping our family together. I never mentioned it, but I always thought about it. I always felt bad about it. Most of my friends were in the same boat. Only two of my friends had both their parents living with them. I did lots of things that caused trouble and pain for my family, although I really did love them. It wasn't their fault that I was unhappy. I got tired of being the problem. I got tired of hurting and tired of hurting them. I caused them to suffer a lot of unhappiness that they didn't deserve..." Arwis' voice trails off as he remembers that fateful night.

***

It is a February 1971 night. Eleven people are present in the Harris apartment in Brownsville, Brooklyn. It is a modest apartment, not lavishly furnished but neat and clean. Hattie Justice, Grace's mother, a short, sweet seventy-year-old silver-haired grandmother, and her granddaughter Christine were visiting from Baltimore. Sonny, the older brother, is also home on leave from the USAF. Clarence, Grace Harris, their five children ranging from three to nine years old, and Terry are there too. The children are running around playing while the others are eating, drinking, and talking.

Grace, talking to her mother, says, "I don't know what I'm going to do with that boy. He's driving us crazy. Every time I turn around, he's in some kind of trouble."

Clarence says, "We don't want to send him to reform school, but if he doesn't stop getting into trouble, that's where he is going to wind up."

Terry chimes in, "Why y'all always picking on me?"

Grace replies, "Nobody's picking on you. You are bringing it on yourself. You failed four subjects in school, you have been caught hooking; I told you to stop running around drinking and smoking pot with those hoodlums. You won't clean your room even; you just don't listen."

"Boy, you been smoking pot?" Hattie questions.

Terry replies, "No, I ain't been smoking no pot."

Grace replies, "Miss Brown told me that she saw you and that Ace smoking pot in her backyard."

Terry, now yelling, replies, "THAT OLD HAG SHOULD MIND HER BUSINESS! SHE'S ALWAYS LYING ABOUT SOMEBODY."

Grace, irked by Terry's behavior, yells back, "DON'T RAISE YOUR VOICE TO ME! SHE IS NOT LYING; PLUS, I SMELLED IT ON YOUR CLOTHES."

"JUST BECAUSE YOU SMELLED IT DOESN'T MEAN I WAS SMOKING IT," Terry retorts.

Clarence replies, "Don't yell at your mother."

Grace, starting to cry but still yelling, says, "SOMETIMES I WISH I NEVER HAD YOU."

An expression that made him look like he had experienced a sharp pain comes on Terry's face. That statement hit him like a ton of bricks; he felt betrayed, alone, hurt, mad, confused, and unwanted all at once. He is visibly shaken.

Hattie says, "Don't say that, Grace."

Grace says, "I mean it. I wish I never had him."

Terry starts to cry. He jumps up from the table, storms into the bathroom, opens the medicine cabinet, and takes every pill in every bottle. Then, he washes his face and tries to compose himself. He comes out of the bathroom and sits back down at the table.

Terry, looking at his mother, thinks, *I really do love you, Mommie. I'm sorry for being such a problem, but I won't be the problem tomorrow.*

Christine gets up and goes into the bathroom. A moment later, she comes back out with some of the empty pill bottles in her hand. Perplexed, she asks, "Aunt Grace, were there any pills in these bottles?"

Grace takes the empty pill bottles and looks at Terry. "Boy, what have you done now?" she says.

Terry feels the room beginning to get darker and darker before he actually falls over onto the floor and starts losing consciousness. He can hear the frenzy in the room.

"Give him a salt solution; it will help to neutralize the pills," Sonny says.

Chris retorts, "No, give him some milk. Milk will coat his stomach."

Grandma says, "Call an ambulance."

Grace replies, "Oh no, he's dying!"

The young ones start to scream and cry.

***

Arwisville is a quiet place, all white and misty like the inside of a large cloud, a place between reality and one's final destination. Terry is one of a crowd that is moving toward an archway; through the archway can be seen two sets of stairs; one that is wide is going down into darkness, and the narrow one is going up and disappearing into a bright light. Thousands are headed down the wide staircase, including pimps, thugs, prostitutes, priests, preachers, lawyers, politicians, murderers, suicides, thieves, adulterers, fornicators, liars, wife-beaters, muggers, and atheists. There are folks from all walks of life, some old, some very young. Terry comes to the archway and looks down into the darkness. An angel is standing there with a large book.

Terry asks, "Am I to be sent down there?"

The angel says, "When will people realize that the gift of life is not to be taken lightly? Life is not to be ended at your whims but according to the plan of the Creator. He had plans for you."

Terry, still looking down into the darkness, says, "So, I'm to be sent down there?"

The angel says, "No, not this time. The only reason you're not being sent down there is that the Boss knows that the reason that you did what you did was to ease the sadness and pain of others. The Creator heard your thoughts as you approached unconsciousness, and he knows that in your heart and mind, you were apologizing to your mother for having caused her and the family so much trouble. That's what saved you. Had your motive been a purely selfish one, you would now be headed for the place of lost souls."

Terry, looking up at the light, says, "So, I'm going up there?"

The angel, writing something in the book, says, "No, your unselfishness has saved you from being sent to the place of lost souls, but it is not time for you to go to your final destination. So, you must go back."

"Go back?" Terry questions.

The angel says, "That's right. I told you that the Creator had plans for you. Had you not come here prematurely, you would have found that out. You now have to go back and dedicate your life to solving the problem that caused you to be here prematurely: the broken family. In ten years, you will become a teacher and marry a woman who has two sons. It will not be easy. As a matter of fact, it will be very difficult. You must know that you can handle it no matter how difficult it is.

105

You will have no recollection of being here until after you have successfully raised your family. Then you will remember being here, and you will then have the knowledge and experience required to establish the Family Restoration Movement. You have been chosen to be the "ARWIS."

Terry, stunned, says, "Family Restoration Movement? The ARWIS?"

The angel replies, "These things will be revealed to you at the proper time. It will happen five years before the new millennium. For the next thirty-four years, you will be tested and trained for the task of establishing this movement. Little by little, over the years, you will come to understand what your mission is. For now, that's all you need to know. It is time for you to go back."

The angel puts his left hand over Terry's heart and touches his forehead with two fingers. Terry closes his eyes.
***

At the FPI Auditorium, Arwis tells the audience, "That's how I became the ARWIS and why I started the Family Restoration Movement."

Kieth says, "Are you telling us this now because of what happened today?"

Arwis replies, "Try not to let what happened today trouble you too much. There are those that are not happy about the progress that you are making and are going to continue to make. Just stay focused. The good thing is that if you all stay focused, the movement cannot be stopped whether I am here or not."

Charles says, "But there is still a lot of work to be done."

Arwis says, "You are well equipped to continue the movement. All you need to do is to stay focused. I promised you that the movement would make great changes in your lives. Well, for those who have joined so far, you have made some changes. What has it done for you?"

Jimmy says, "With your help, we have developed strategies for creating success in our families by prioritizing our lives instead of allowing ourselves to have our priorities dictated to us by the system like we had been doing for far too long."

Kieth says, "We are no longer slaves to trends and fads, which actually program us to spend our money frivolously and wastefully. We have developed selective purchasing and spending habits. We are no longer allowing ourselves to be programmed into being walking billboards, tricked into wanting and spending so much time, energy, effort, and money on having the latest designer, this or that which we really don't need. We now know that the designers themselves don't wear those expensive clothes that they sell us. They don't want or need to wear them. What they want and need is to sell them to us so that they can use our money to better their lives and the lives of their families."

Mr. Evans says, "We have become frugal. For example, we plan to go for two solid years without buying any new clothes whatsoever. We have created our own fads, and we see huge balances in our bank accounts as a result. We have meals together as much as possible, which affords us much-needed quality time together and makes good economic sense. We are closer and happier with each other because we are experiencing a collective effort to accomplish our economic goals. Sacrificing, growing, and learning together make our families stronger and more viable. Soon, we will be, in large numbers, able to afford the houses that we do need."

"Being involved with the Family Restoration Movement has made a serious difference in the lives of our families. We have made some major changes in how we live and what we consider important. Some changes have been simple; some not so simple, but all have had hugely significant results," Mr. Carter adds.

Danny Delainie says, "We pray together. Whatever our religious beliefs, we give thanks for our lives, our families, FPI, and our second chance. We ask the Creator for his continued guidance and blessings, and we never argue or fight around our children. We know that we have to set good examples for them."

Michael speaks up, saying, "We monitor and censor what our children see and hear on radio, TV, and the internet.

We know that what our children see and hear influences what they say and do."

Donald adds, "We're practicing being truthful and honest. We've accepted honesty as the best policy. We're moderate in our indulgences. We recognize our bodies as our temples, and again, we must set good examples for our children."

Karen joins in, too. "We read to our children every day, even if it's just one sentence. We take an active part in their academic, moral, and spiritual development. We're involved in the dictionary transcription project together. We define and study at least five words per day. We are growing in knowledge together and at no cost." (A gift from Malcolm X.)

Shamelle says, "We save or invest some amount of money every week without fail. We listen more to our mates and children. We know the importance of communication, of sharing and respecting each other's thoughts, ideas, and feelings."

Re-Pete, too, chimes in. "We have taken the N---- word out of our vocabularies. No longer will we be psyched into degrading our own people, and we reaffirm on a daily basis our commitment to the movement. FATHER AND MOTHER, I LOVE YOU."

When Arwis begins his last talk with this group of Movementors, he starts off by saying, "Education is the key. You hear it over and over and over. But what does that really mean? The kind of education that folks need will leave them with a clear understanding of the four mathematical procedures and the functions of all of the members of those procedures, the functions of the eight parts of speech, and the four sentence types. This information is something that all should have at this point. But you will be hard-pressed to find anyone who remembers all of these fundamentals. Statistics say that the reading and math scores of children today are horrendous. Sad but true. The real sad truth is that it is by design. There are essential basics that were not and are still not being taught the way that they should be taught."

Arwis looks around the group as he continues, "These fundamentals are the foundation of English and Math. You must know them so that going forward, you will be able to comprehend just about anything that you read. There are laws on the books that govern your behavior that you cannot understand. Learning and knowing your math and English fundamentals will help to change that. This directive is for all parents and children alike. For literally hundreds of years, people of color were cheated when it came to education, and We're still playing catch up."

He pauses to let that statement sink in before continuing, "When blacks were brought to this country, they were not allowed to learn to read or write. This was done on purpose. Black people were to be obedient, not educated. After the slaves were freed, they were allowed to pursue education, but the schools, the curriculum, and the method of teaching were controlled by the slave owners. Black children were not given the same information that others were given. For example, if a subject contained seven steps, we were given 1,2,4,5,7, which left gaps in our understanding. Same with Mathematics. We were not taught all of the names and functions of the members of the four mathematical procedures. Here are some fundamentals of Mathematics. I call these digits the alphabet of Math: 0,1,2,3,4,5,6,7,8,9. We use them in our four mathematical procedures. Multiplication, Division, Addition, Subtraction," Arwis looks at each person standing before him before continuing.

"Every position in these procedures has a name and a function. Knowing this information will greatly increase your understanding of and improve your skill with mathematical procedures. Fractions, Geometry, Algebra, Trigonometry, etc. Your fear or dislike of math is really because of the way you think about math. You think about it based on what knowledge you have, which does not include the names and functions of the positions in the math procedures. Not knowing these fundamentals is a (the) problem. Math is the second most important subject on this planet, and YOU are supposed to know its fundamentals. Familiarize yourself with these fundamentals, which will definitely help you to be more proficient with math. As for the English language, Important fundamentals of English are the eight parts of speech and the four sentence types," Arwis smiles as he explains to the group.

"I will be leaving soon, but I have, through FPI, established a secondary education program, " he continued. It is basically a refresher course in Math and English, and it's called "refresh ME," and the "ME" is Math and English. It's a program that anyone interested in improving their quality of life can come to and get refreshed on these extremely important basic fundamentals of grammar and mathematics. All who become involved will improve the quality of their life because they will know better how to decipher more written information, which will allow them to be more successful," he stops as he hears murmurs of excitement from the group.

"But they must know the fundamentals well; otherwise, they can't really understand or take advantage of many of the opportunities that exist because they don't understand them written," he cautions them, smiling. "Our kids listen to rap songs, some of which have over 1000 words. And they can sync right along with it. Word for word. Now, if you turn it on in the middle, they'll pick it up from there and finish. My point is that if they can learn and retain that much information rhythmically and accurately, then they can certainly retain the information that is the functions of the eight parts of speech, which are more important than the first 1000 words of any rap song. Reading, writing, and arithmetic is what the world functions on, so let's get it together. You can't do them well without the fundamentals. So, be ready to sign up for the program when it comes to your neighborhood. 'Refresh ME'. Tell your friends and family about the program. Everyone can use a refresher In Math and English. No one should be afraid of fractions or decimals or geometry or algebra. No one, and if they know the fundamentals, the procedures become very simple."

As he concludes his speech, Arwis says, "Always remember that a united family is a formidable entity that is hard to beat. It will prosper. It will be successful in spite of all the obstacles that are put in its way. The family is the first institution put in place by the Creator, and it is of great importance to keep it together. Now, I want this to be clearly understood; ideally, having the family living and growing together is best. However, sometimes, the father and mother have differences that will not allow them to live together. In both scenarios, the important thing is that there is Love, Understanding, and cooperation between the family members. This will make for a successful family regardless of the proximity of the members. Practice these methods for at least one year, and they will perpetuate success in your families indefinitely."

The audience applauds.

***

At the Di'Marco Mansion at night, Vincent Di'Marco, the refuted head of an organized crime family, has assembled a group of ten of his business associates who are seated around a large table in the lavishly furnished meeting room of his mansion.

Di'Marco says, "I want to thank you all for showing your concern for my son. As you know, he is very sick, and the only hope for him is to have a blood transfusion. Due to complications, I cannot be his donor. There were only two other people in this country with this rare blood type. We found out that the one who lived in Arizona died last month."

"What about the other one?" Associate 2 questions.

Di'Marco says, "He has not been found yet. The doctors know his name, but they don't know where he is. That is why I asked you all to come here tonight. I want to ask you all to use all of your sources to locate this man. His name is Terry Harris. His last known address is in Brooklyn."

Associate 3 adds, "How long does your son have?"

Di'Marco replies, "The doctors say two or three weeks at the most. I regret to say that the business that was planned for tonight must be postponed until a later date. I need to spend as much time as I can with my son. I'm sorry, but I cannot concentrate on anything right now. I'm sure you all understand. The business will keep."

The men all gesture in agreement. They all rise, each giving hugs, kisses on each cheek, and words of encouragement to Di'Marco before they leave. Gennelli, who has been standing at attention behind Di'Marco's chair, is the last to leave the room. He stops at the door and looks back at Di'Marco, who has sat back down again and cradled his head in his hands.

Gennelli says, "Don't worry, Mr. D. The boys will find this Terry Harris, and your boy will be fine."

Di'Marco replies, "Bring the car around."

Gennelli says, "Sure, boss, right away."

Gennelli leaves the room.

***

At the hotel room later that night, Arwis is seen seated in a chair, resting his head back and looking through the open terrace doors at the lights of the city. The television is on and tuned to the Channel Seven news broadcast. We hear the voice of the news commentator.

"The mayor has given his approval for the family advocate school days program proposed by FPI, the Family Promoters Co., to be implemented in New York City public schools. The family advocates program, which has been sanctioned by hundreds of employers, will allow two (2) "school days" per year, with pay, for working parents with children in school. These two days will be used as four (4) half days spread out over the school year. (For example, one half-day every 75 days) in a manner that a parent will work in his child's school in the morning and report to his regular job in the afternoon. Another parent will work at his regular job in the morning and report to the school that afternoon. Employers who participate in the program will receive a tax break to offset any loss in productivity. The mayor feels that this program will literally utilize thousands of parents, including social service recipient parents, in a place where their skills and talents would do an enormous amount of good for the schools, the parents themselves, the children, and the city. A spokesman for FPI said that one of the main functions of the family advocates in the program would be to serve as interpreters for the many different immigrant parents."

Arwis looks over at the TV and smiles; the news commentator continues to say, "We switch you now to Lonny Johnson reporting from Mt. Sanai Hospital."

Lonny takes over. "This is Lonny Johnson in front of Mt. Sanai Hospital, where refuted crime lord Vincent Di'Marco has just left after a visit with his seven-year-old son, who has taken a turn for the worse."

Johnson turns and points to Di'Marco's limousine, which is seen in the background, pulling away from the hospital. Johnson turns back to the camera and continues.

"Young Steven is reported to be suffering from a rare disease of the blood, and doctors say that there is little hope that he will survive unless he receives a complete blood transfusion. The problem is that Mr. Di'Marco cannot give his son the transfusion that he needs because two years ago, he was diagnosed as having a mild strain of the HIV virus. There were only two other people in this country who had this rare blood type: ABO-positive. Our sources have found that one of them, a man living in Phoenix, Arizona, died last month in a car accident, and the other person with this rare blood type has not yet been found. This is a very sad case of affairs. This man is said to be worth four and one half billion dollars, and he finds himself helpless when it comes to saving the life of his only son. Sad, very sad. This is Lonny Johnson reporting live from Mt. Sanai Hospital."

Arwis reaches over and picks up the remote from the table next to his chair. He pauses and looks at the remote control. He stands up and turns off the TV, goes over, and falls backward onto his bed. He lies down for a few minutes, just looking up at the ceiling. He then slowly closes his eyes and drifts off to sleep.

At Di'Marco's home in the morning, Di'Marco is sitting right in the center of a beautiful sprawling piece of property that resembles a golf course in its sculptured landscape. At first light, Mr. Di'Marco, in his pajamas, is standing at his bedroom window looking out. He sees the first rays of the sun dancing through the leaves on the trees. He's holding a picture of his wife and son. He walks over, opens his bedroom door, and steps into the hall, calling Gennelli.

Di'Marco says, "Gennelli, bring the car around in fifteen minutes. We're going to the hospital."

Gennelli replies, yelling, "Right, Mr. D. Fifteen minutes."

Di'Marco is seen coming out of his house and getting into his car. The car pulls out of the driveway and heads for the city. As the car turns onto the L.I.E headed west, we can see the skyline of the city way off in the distance. Di'Marco pulls up in front of Mt. Sanai Hospital, and Gennelli and Di'Marco exit the car, entering the hospital.

Steven Di'Marco sees his father coming into his room. Gennelli is waiting in the hallway. Di'Marco walks over to his son's bed and kisses him on the forehead. He then says, "How are you feeling this morning, Son?"

Steven replies, "Okay, I guess. Why don't you just take me home, Dad? They're not gonna find the right blood for me. I know I'm gonna die. It's alright, Dad, but if I'm gonna die, I want to die in my own bed."

Di'Marco, swallowing hard as if trying hard not to let his emotions show, says, "Don't say that, Steven. You're not going to die. They're gonna find it. You hang in there. I promise you; they'll find it."

Steven responds, "I'm not afraid anymore, Dad."

Di'Marco says, "There's no reason for you to be afraid, Steven. Everything's gonna be fine; you just wait and see."

Gennelli sticks his head in the door and says, "There's two moolies out here to see you, Mr. D."

Di'Marco replies, "You know that I don't like that word, Gennelli. Who are they? I'll be right back, Son."

Di'Marco steps into the hallway to see who it is. Arwis and one of the movementors are waiting to speak to him. The movementor is looking at Gennelli very hard and trying to place him. He remembers seeing Gennelli talking to Mason just before Mason entered the FPI building and made an attempt to shoot Arwis. He whispers into Arwis's ear.

Di'Marco speaks, saying, "What can I do for you?"

Arwis replies, "It's about what I can do for you. My friend here is positive that he saw this fellow talking to a man who made an attempt on my life."

Di'Marco says, "Are you Arwis?"

Arwis nods in the affirmative.

Di'Marco says, "Your... What d'ya call it...? Yeah, 'movement' is costing me and my associates a lot of money, but this is not the time or place to talk about that. Why are you here?"

Arwis replies, "I can't say that I'm sorry about that. Actually, this is only the beginning. Times are changing, Mr. Di'Marco, but you're right; this is not the time or place to talk about that."

Their eyes meet for a long moment, then Arwis speaks. "I need to speak to you in private."

Gennelli gestures a protest, but Mr. Di'Marco puts his hand out to stop him. Gennelli murmurs, "But, boss—"

Di'Marco, still looking at Arwis, says, "It's okay; it's okay."

Di'Marco takes Arwis into the empty room across from his son's room, then says, "Okay, what do you want?"

Arwis says, "I didn't realize until now that you were the one who sent that killer after me. We thought that it may have been a government man. You may be glad that he didn't kill me."

Di'Marco, his forehead furrowed, asks, "And just why should I be glad of that? Look, what is this all about?"

Arwis walks over and looks out of the window. He turns to Di'Marco and says, "I'm called Arwis, but my name is Terry Harris."

Di'Marco, kind of annoyed, replies with an attitude, "So what? What does that have to..." He trails off and pauses. "Terry Harris? ABO positive?"

Arwis, nodding an affirmative, slightly smiles. Their eyes meet and hold for a long moment. Di'Marco's eyes well up with tears; he looks across the hall at his son and then back at Arwis.

Di'Marco goes on to say, "Alright, name your price."

Stunned, Arwis asks, "My price?" He looks like he feels he has been insulted, but he feels pity for Di'Marco.

Di'Marco once again says, "How much do you want to save my son? How much do you want to do the transfusion?"

Arwis says, "I'm sorry, Mr. Di'Marco, I didn't come here to sell you anything."

Somewhat surprised, Di'Marco questions, "Then why did you come? To gloat? Is that it? If you didn't come to sell me your blood, then why did you come?"

Arwis replies, "I came to help a little boy have the chance to grow up and to give you a chance to see a sonrise. I couldn't put a price tag on a little boy's life. I'm just glad that I can be here for him."

Di'Marco, growing more surprised and confused, says, "I don't understand you. You mean you didn't come to ask for any money? And you're willing to help my son even after you found out that I was the one who tried to have you killed?"

Arwis says, "No, I didn't come to ask for money, and I didn't know until I got here that you were the one who sent a hit man after me, but he didn't shoot me, so that's neither here nor there. I'm willing to help a son rise because I can. I understand that you are worth a great deal of money, but you couldn't transfuse your boy with it, and I don't have the right to put a price tag on his life. As a father, I understand the importance of a son as being the next generation, the future of the family."

Di'Marco just stands there looking at Arwis with a blank stare on his face.

Arwis says, "Not only do I not want any money, but I also don't want any publicity either. Not everyone would agree with my decision to do this. I suspect that there would be opposition from your people and mine. In case you haven't noticed, I'm black. But be that as it may, if you still want to save your son, my blood can do it, and my spirit is willing."

Di'Marco says, "It wouldn't matter to me if you were green. All I care about is saving my boy's life."

Arwis, satisfied, says, "Then call his doctors, and let's get it done."

Their eyes meet again, both of their faces solemn, but then a slight smile breaks at the corner of Arwis's mouth, and then one appears on Di'Marco's face.

Di'Marco rushes out of the room past Gennelli toward his son's room. He rushes into his son's room, tears rolling down his face, but with a big smile spread on his lips. Steven looks up and sees the joy on his father's face. Surprised, he asks, "Dad, you found him, didn't you? I know you did; that's why you're so happy, right? I'm not gonna die?"

"I told you I would find. I told you not to worry. You're going to be fine, son. Everything is gonna be fine!" Di'Marco says excitedly.

Di'Marco lifts his son into his arms and hugs him, tears still flowing down his face. Steven embraces his father.

Looking up, Di'Marco prays, "Thank you, God. Thank you..." Then he looks at his son, eyes drowning in happy tears, and says, "I love you, Son. I love you..."

Gennelli is watching everything with a perplexed and angry look on his face. He looks back and forth from Arwis, who is in the hallway adjacent to Steven Di'Marco's room.

***

Arwis walks over to Gennelli and says, All human blood is red, every human life is precious! and our objective in life is to see another sonrise.

'Chicago Board of Education' is what the name on the top of the building reads. In the conference room inside, a panel of representatives from several Chicago schools is seated at a large, polished mahogany table with high-backed chairs, sipping coffee and making small talk. The seat at the head of the table is empty. A cluster of glasses, some napkins, and a pitcher of water are in the center of the table. Manila folders have been placed on the table in front of each chair. A woman comes into the room and sits in the empty chair at the head of the table, beginning to speak.

"Good morning. Shall we get started?" Miss Davis says.

The panel returns her greeting and begins to open their folders.

Miss Davis continues, "What you have in front of you are the reading scores of 60 students as of the close of school in June and the scores from the battery of tests given two weeks ago. As you can see, the scores have changed dramatically."

The last man seated at the table lifts his head and smiles; it's none other than Arwis.

What do you think would happen if men stopped mistreating their children and their wives?

Started enriching their lives, stopped so much getting high, and started making great strides.

What do you think would happen?

What do you think?

What do you think what happened if the brothers really started building?

I mean, started spending more quality time with their children,

Started bringing out all of their children's good, just like Earl did for Tiger Woods.

Everybody's hip to what Joe Jackson did.

This brother had a vision for five of his kids.

And you know, Mr. Williams, behind Serena and Venus,

Took his girls to the top of the game of tennis.

And behind Michael Jordan, pop Jordan stood tall,

Helped his son might become the king of basketball.

It's time for more black fathers to make that move.

Come on, brothers, let's get in the groove.

What do you think?

What do you think would happen if instead of wasting their money on cocaine rocks, brothers started investing in bonds and stocks?

Started pooling their resources?

I mean, finally really joining forces to make life better for our families,

Staying out of jails and penitentiaries.

What do you think would happen?

What do you think?

I really think we can do this.

And with God's help, ain't nothing to this.

Or would you rather keep being played?

Come on brothers. Let's try and see.

Let's really start focusing on God and family.

What do you think?

Check it out. Brothers. Can't you see it?

Anything we want our kids to be?

With our help. They can be it.

What do you think?

What do you think would happen if you realize that this is true?

Well, it is. It really is.

So, what are you going to do?

What do you think?

ABOUT AUTHOR

Sherman Terry Lewis says that as a father and family man, I will – **A**lways **R**eap **W**hat **I** **S**ew!

THE END